The Tutor's Handbook
MATH
Grade 5

Written by Peter Riopel

Illustrated by Margeaux Lucas

Project Manager: Kathleen Hex
Editor: Michael Batty
Introduction: Carol Wright
Book Design: Rita Hudson
Cover Design: Riley Wilkinson
Graphic Artist: Randy Shinsato
Cover Photos: Anthony Nex Photography

FS122133 The Tutor's Handbook: Math Grade 5
All rights reserved—Printed in the U.S.A.
23740 Hawthorne Blvd., Torrance, CA 90505

Notice! Pages may be reproduced for classroom or home use only, not for commercial resale. No part of this publication may be reproduced for storage in a retrieval system, or transmitted in any form or by any means—electronic, mechanical, recording, etc.—without the prior written permission of the publisher. Reproduction of these materials for an entire school or school system is strictly prohibited.

Copyright © 2001 Frank Schaffer Publications, Inc.

TABLE OF CONTENTS

Tutors as Coaches 3

Grade Level Expectations 4

The Tutoring Session 6

Strategies for Success 8

Student Survey (Beginning) 9

Making Connections 10

Numbers and Computation 12
    Numbers and Computation (Pretest) 15
    Using Decimals (Numbers and Computation) 16
    Using Fractions (Numbers and Computation) 17
    Numbers and Computation (Posttest) 18

Patterns 19
    Patterns (Pretest) 22
    Number Patterns (Patterns) 23
    Predictable Patterns (Patterns) 24
    Patterns Practice (Patterns) 25
    Patterns (Posttest) 26

Geometry 27
    Geometry (Pretest) 29
    Shapes and Symmetry (Geometry) 30
    Coordinate Graphing (Geometry) 31
    Congruent Figures (Geometry) 32
    Geometry (Posttest) 33

Measurement 34
    Measurement (Pretest) 37
    Metric Measurement (Measurement) 38
    U.S. Customary Units (Measurement) 39

    Other U.S. Customary Units (Measurement) 40
    Measurement (Posttest) 41

Data Analysis, Statistics, and Probability 42
    Data Analysis, Statistics, and Probability (Pretest) 45
    Pizza Palace (Data Analysis, Statistics, and Probability) 46
    Number Roll (Data Analysis, Statistics, and Probability) 47
    Graphs and Averages (Data Analysis, Statistics, and Probability) 48
    Data Analysis, Statistics, and Probability (Posttest) 49

Problem Solving 50
    Problem Solving (Pretest) 51
    School Days (Problem Solving) 52
    Word Problems (Problem Solving) 53
    Missing Information (Problem Solving) 54
    Problem Solving (Posttest) 55

Let's Review (Numbers and Computation) 56

Let's Review (Patterns) 57

Let's Review (Geometry) 58

Let's Review (Measurement) 59

Let's Review (Data Analysis, Statistics, and Probability) 60

Let's Review (Problem Solving) 61

Student Survey (Final) 62

Answers 63

TUTORS AS COACHES

As a tutor for a young child, consider your role as that of a coach. Picture the coaches you have seen running along the sidelines at local soccer games. They believe in their teams. They encourage, support, advise, and challenge to help their teams achieve victory. As a tutor, you will assume a similar role as you help the child achieve success in fifth grade math activities.

Patience

Probably one of the most important qualities in a coach or tutor is patience. You have a clear understanding of the math concepts you will be helping the child develop. However, the student will not master these skills overnight. Allow the child sufficient time to explore and practice each skill you present.

Enthusiasm

Just like an athletic coach, the tutor must convey to the student a belief in his or her ability to master the skills. Be an encourager! Call attention to the progress that the child is making in math. Your sincere praise will help the child feel comfortable taking risks and may help him or her develop confidence with math activities.

Process

Soccer coaches are obviously focused on helping their teams win. If you look closely, you will notice that coaches actually spend much of the time helping the players learn the process of winning a game. As you help the student develop a variety of math strategies, try to focus a significant amount of energy on the things the child is doing to solve the problems. Encourage the student to talk out loud as he or she thinks about and works on a problem. Pose thoughtful questions about the process used to solve a problem. This is more helpful than simply marking answers right or wrong.

Make it a common practice to ask the child to tell you how he or she got the answer to a problem. If you discover the child began solving an addition problem in the tens place, ask the child why he or she began that way. Just as the athletic coach does not allow the team to practice over and over the wrong way to play, help the student succeed by talking about the process that will help him or her reach the correct answer. Resist the temptation to just tell the student the correct answer as this will result in little long term learning. Pose questions about the problem that will challenge the child to explore and utilize the different strategies he or she is developing. When the child correctly solves a problem, encourage him or her to describe the process used to solve it.

In your important role of tutor as coach, have patience with the student! Remember that the child is learning as fast as he or she can. Be enthusiastic about learning! Your excitement and encouragement may help the child improve his or her attitude toward math. Finally, focus on the process of learning! It is just as important as getting the right answer.

GRADE LEVEL EXPECTATIONS

The following grade level expectations are based on national math standards as set by the National Council of Teachers of Mathematics.

Numbers and Computation

Fifth graders should be able to

- understand place value through billions
- add and subtract whole numbers through millions with and without regrouping
- multiply and divide with three digit numbers
- add, subtract, multiply, and divide with decimals to thousandths
- find equivalent forms of fractions, decimals, and percents (½ = .50 = 50%)
- compare and order fractions and decimals
- add and subtract fractions and mixed numbers with like and unlike denominators
- convert mixed numbers to fractions and fractions to mixed numbers
- estimate and round whole numbers, decimals, and fractions

Geometry

Fifth graders should be able to

- identify, describe, and classify two- and three-dimensional shapes: triangles, circles, quadrilaterals, polygons, prisms, pyramid, cone, cylinder, and sphere
- identify the line of symmetry
- identify or predict the results of flips, slides, and turns
- use ordered pairs on a coordinate grid
- understand geometric vocabulary

Patterns

Fifth graders should be able to

- identify, describe, and extend geometric and numeric patterns
- use patterns to predict outcomes
- identify and describe patterns using tables and graphs
- find relationships between quantities to aid problem solving

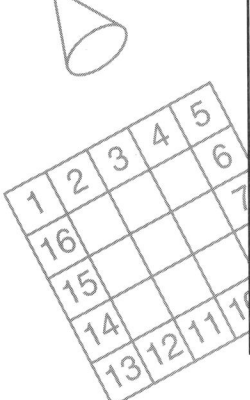

GRADE LEVEL EXPECTATIONS

Data Analysis, Statistics, and Probability
Fifth graders should be able to

- collect and organize data
- create and interpret tables and graphs: bar graphs, line graphs, circle graphs, and pictographs
- find averages
- make predictions based on data
- determine the probability of an event and describe it as *certain, equally likely,* or *impossible*
- represent the likelihood of an event as a number between 0 and 1

Measurement
Fifth graders should be able to

- use measurements in U.S. customary and metric systems
- identify and apply correct U.S. customary or metric units of measurement
- estimate measurements
- make conversions within a system of measurement
- find area, perimeter, and volume of shapes using formulas
- calculate hours and minutes of elapsed time

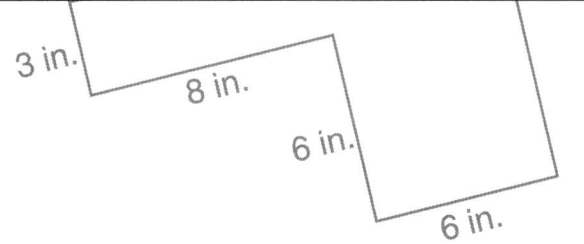

Problem Solving
Fifth graders should be able to

- identify the appropriate operation for solving a problem
- use a variety of strategies for problem solving
- identify necessary and unnecessary information
- evaluate and explain the problem-solving process used

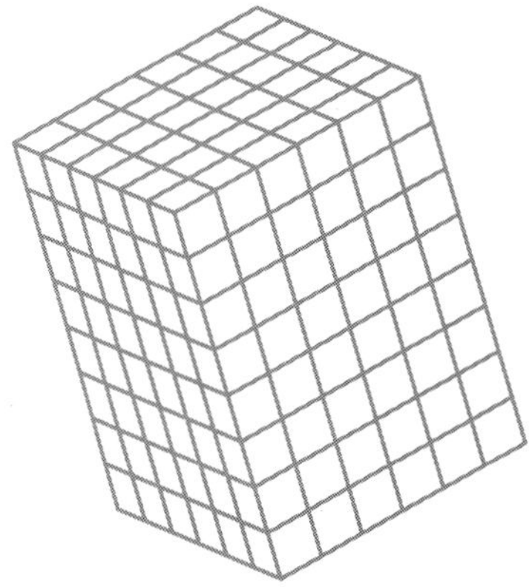

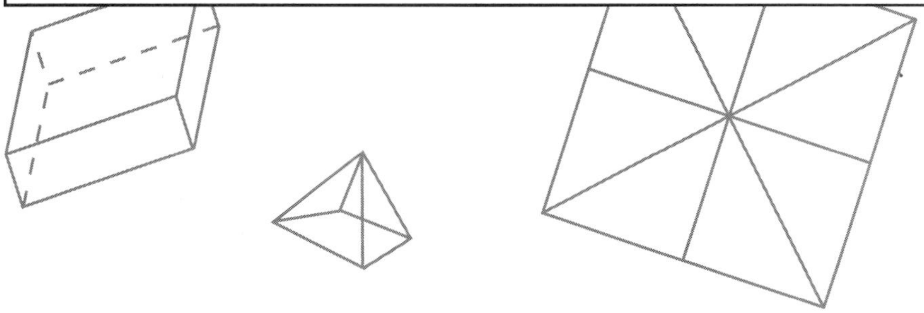

THE TUTORING SESSION

Getting Started

At the beginning of a session, discuss with the student what the two of you hope to accomplish. Allow the student to help decide what should be achieved during the session. Whatever concerns the student—that night's homework, an upcoming test, or a concept covered in class that seemed unclear—should probably be addressed first. Ask the student, "How may I help you today?" Establish goals for the session and be sure that the goals are worthwhile.

Make your process and method apparent to the student. Do you prefer to work right through a page of problems and then correct and review, or to discuss the problems as you go, diverging as necessary? If you have specific rules or policies, state these clearly.

Assessing the Student's Needs

The student survey on page 9 contains open-ended questions to solicit statements from the student about his or her ability in and perception of math. Observe the student closely as he or she answers these questions to determine his or her attitude.

Helpful Hint: Keep a list of all specific skills that need improvement. Some of these will become apparent in pretests, and some will show up as you work with the student.

Each section of this book includes a pretest. Solving problems in the pretests typically involves several skills, so note not only which problems the student misses, but also which specific skills show weakness in the missed problems.

Review

Briefly reviewing types of problems worked on in the previous session is often a good idea. You might say, "Remember the division problems that had a zero in the quotient? These were a little confusing at first, but then you learned how to do that type of problem. Here's one like it. Let's see if you can still do it." In the previous session, you might have asked the student to determine how close a snail would be to a house after three hours if it started four feet away and crawled one-half foot per hour. To follow up, you might say, "Remember that snail? What if it started at the same place, four feet from the house, but this time crawled two feet every three hours? How far from the house would it be after four hours?"

Helpful Hint: When beginning instruction in a new concept, problems might appear in areas that you thought had been mastered. Review these concepts again with the student.

A student may see review as unnecessary repetition of topics already covered. Keep it interesting by integrating review into other work. For example, if the student needs more practice in multiplying decimals and he or she is working on the area of rectangles, present a rectangle's dimensions in decimal measurements (for example, 3.7 cm x 4.5 cm).

© 2001 Frank Schaffer Publications, Inc.   FS122133 The Tutor's Handbook: Math Grade 5

THE TUTORING SESSION

Introducing New Concepts

When introducing new concepts, start with manipulatives (hands-on materials), if possible. Many concepts at this grade level can be demonstrated with models, paper cutouts, or activities. To introduce fractions, for example, use circles made of colored construction paper and have the student cut them into fractional pieces. Allow him or her to use the pieces when working out written problems.

Helpful Hint: Be patient. Don't progress to harder problems too quickly. What may seem repetitious and boring to you might please the student.

If the student becomes frustrated or encounters a difficult problem, acknowledge the difficulty and remind him or her that each new concept will seem impossible at first but become clear, and even easy, with practice.

Practice Makes Perfect

Provide the child with several opportunities to practice the new concepts with your guidance. The practice pages included in this book can be used to create a multitude of practice opportunities. Allow the child plenty of time to work out the problems and provide assistance when needed. Frequently, but gently, remind the student of the strategies he or she has learned that can be applied to this concept.

Ending the Session

At the end of a session, ask the student to summarize what was covered. He or she should be able to describe what was learned. It is constructive to make the student aware of his or her progress and of the strategy of the session.

If independent activities are assigned, make sure the child has the necessary tools to complete the work. Ask the child to show you how he or she will complete the problems. You can intercept any difficulties, answer any questions, and help ensure success on the assignment.

Finally, end the session on a positive note. Congratulate the student on a job well done and encourage him or her to continue doing his or her best.

STRATEGIES FOR SUCCESS

Scheduling an appropriate hour for the tutoring session can have a great influence on the student's success. While your availability and the parent and child's schedules are limiting factors, try to choose a time of day in which you will have the student's full attention. Some students work best immediately after school, but others need a break and a snack first.

When you are helping the student with his or her work, be careful to not do too much for him or her. If you get the answer before the student, patience can be difficult, and you may find yourself wanting to hurry things along. On difficult exercises, most students will let you do as much of the work as you are willing to. Your role as tutor is to help the child learn to accomplish math tasks independently.

When you are working on a problem with the student, you are serving as a model. Verbalize what you are doing and show the student how you organize your work on paper. For example, if you were listing the numbers $1\frac{3}{4}$, $1\frac{7}{5}$, and $4\frac{1}{3}$ in order from least to greatest, you might say, "Two of the numbers are written as fractions but are greater than one whole, so I will change them to mixed numbers. Now I see that $4\frac{1}{3}$ is the largest. Now what about the other two numbers? When I am not sure what to do, I try restating the problem to myself. Which is bigger, $2\frac{1}{4}$ or $2\frac{2}{5}$? How do I compare $\frac{1}{4}$ and $\frac{2}{5}$?"

If the student seems to be guessing, instead of answering the question, ask why he or she thinks that what he or she is suggesting is correct. Often, being asked to explain focuses the student's attention on the details of a problem and enables him or her to see the process more clearly.

> **Helpful Hint:** When you write examples or instructional notes, take the time to print clearly and neatly. Model the importance of good organization in math.

If you will be traveling to the student's home, think about what you will bring. You may not know what the student is currently studying in school and thus need to be prepared for any math concept. Your tutoring bag might contain paper (binder, graph, scratch, construction), pencils (#2, colored), geometry implements (compass, protractor, metric, and customary rulers), a hole punch, scissors, a large eraser, flash cards, correction fluid, timed tests for multiplication and division, manipulatives (geoboard, pattern blocks, number chart, multiplication chart), and your appointment calendar.

> **Helpful Hint:** Learning math can be stressful for the student. Humor is a good antidote for stress. Be careful to not inadvertently criticize; you are trying to build confidence.

If you vary activities during the session, time will seem to pass quickly for the student. You can vary activities by switching between manipulatives and problems on paper. Or you can alternate between a couple of paper problems and a couple of problems from a math textbook. Just as many problems can be done in an hour this way, but to the student it will seem like less work than doing a full page all at once.

Try asking the student to give you a problem. Some students enjoy the idea of turning the tables on the tutor. This is an effective way to check the student's understanding, as it takes a better understanding of math concepts to write problems than to work them.

Student _____ Beginning

Student Survey

Use these questions as a guide when initiating discussion with the student. It is not important to get an answer to each, but rather to get the child to discuss his or her perceptions of math. Space is provided to make notes on the child's remarks. Allow the student time to think and to explain his or her responses. Save these notes for future reference.

1 When you think about doing math, how do you feel?

2 Why have you come to math tutoring?

3 If you thought about which subjects you like best, how would math rate?

4 What is your favorite thing about math?

5 What do you like least about math?

6 What do you think the math tutoring will be like?

As the child answered these questions, what did you notice?

© 2001 Frank Schaffer Publications, Inc. FS122133 The Tutor's Handbook: Math Grade 5

MAKING CONNECTIONS

Math is not an isolated, academic exercise found only in textbooks, but a way to describe the physical relationships of things all around us. The following are ways in which you might show a student that math surrounds him or her.

Math All Around Us

Math is everywhere in the student's home. The student might find a package of 250 napkins in a kitchen cabinet. How long might they last? Have the student tally napkin use in the house, find the average daily use, and divide that average into the number of napkins. How many napkins are left in the opened package? Is it ⅔ full? How many napkins out of 250 is that?

Have the student look at the price on a youth magazine. If one issue costs $2.75, what would a year's subscription cost? What is the price per page? If the student receives a discount of ⅓ off the subscription, how much does he or she pay?

Wrenches and sockets come in sets organized by size, in either standard or metric units. Try removing all of the sockets from a set, mixing them up, and asking the student to replace them in order.

Similar patterns can be found on clocks. How many times per day will the hour hand and minute hand form a right angle? Three o'clock looks like the fraction ¼ would on a circle. Four o'clock looks like ⅓. Which time of day looks like ⅔?

Have the student look at packages of food in the kitchen that have weights in ounces or grams and that have prices on them. Some packages of the same item may have the same weight but different prices. Some packages may have a lower price but use a package that is one ounce smaller. Is that package a good buy? If the student bought a large quantity, would he or she save money?

Thermometers provide a good demonstration of range. If the temperature outside was 50°F and dropped 20 degrees, the current temperature would be 2 degrees below freezing. Have the student compare Fahrenheit and Celsius. What temperature ranges on each scale would be comfortable for a person?

Flower pots are measured by diameter. Which diameter is measured, the top or bottom? Why are pots measured like this? How much more soil would be needed to fill a six-inch pot than a four-inch pot?

Some banks will provide a sample or introductory checkbook. Create a fictional account for your student and provide instruction on writing checks. You might have to show the student the correct spellings of numbers. Some people make small errors when writing checks, such as putting a decimal over 100 when writing cents (for example, .⁴⁹⁄₁₀₀). Give the student a fictional million dollars and have him or her write checks and keep a check register. Let the student "buy" dream items. Can the student correctly write a check for the cost of a sports car? Can he or she subtract that amount from one million? Can the student find items with costs that total exactly $1,000,000?

MAKING CONNECTIONS

Language Arts Connections

Practice finding averages with the student's favorite book. Ask the child to count the number of words on a page. Repeat for several pages. Then he or she can calculate the average number of words per page.

Make a graph of frequently occurring words. Encourage the student to read several pages from a book, magazine, or newspaper. He or she should write a list of the ten words that he or she thinks occur most frequently in that passage. Return to the reading and have the child count and tally each time the word occurs in the passage. Help the student create a graph of the results.

LITERATURE LIST

MULTIPLICATION AND DIVISION

The Doorbell Rang by Pat Hutchins (Mulberry Books, 1986).

A Remainder of One by Elinor Pinczes (Houghton Mifflin, 1995).

MONEY

The Story of Money by Betsy and Guilio Maestro (Houghton Mifflin, 1995).

Alexander, Who Used to be Rich Last Sunday by Judith Viorst (Simon and Schuster, 1980).

GEOMETRY

Grandfather Tang's Story by Ann Tompert (Crown Publishing Group, 1997).

PLACE VALUE

How Much is a Million? by David M. Schwartz (Morrow, William and Co., 1993).

FRACTIONS

How Pizza Came to Queens by Dayal Kaur Kalsa (Crown Books for Young Readers, 1989).

MEASUREMENT

Math Curse by Jon Scieszka (Viking Children's Books, 1995).

PATTERNS

The King's Chessboard by David Birch (Dial, 1988).

Science Connections

Have the student research the distances between planets in our solar system. Use these distances to create word problems for the student to solve. For example: Mercury is (on average) 36 million miles from the sun and Jupiter is (on average) 483.4 million miles from the sun. What is the distance between Mercury and Jupiter?

Social Studies Connections

Just as the post office and phone companies use numbering systems, so do our interstate freeway systems. Generally, north-south routes have odd numbers and east-west routes have even numbers. Major routes are usually one- or two-digit numbers. Alternate routes usually have three-digit numbers, with principal routes included in the tens and ones places.

Ask the student to tell you about important events during his or her favorite period in history. Find mathematical elements and create problem-solving opportunities. For example, if the student enjoys history of ancient Egypt, devise a question about the shape and volume of pyramids.

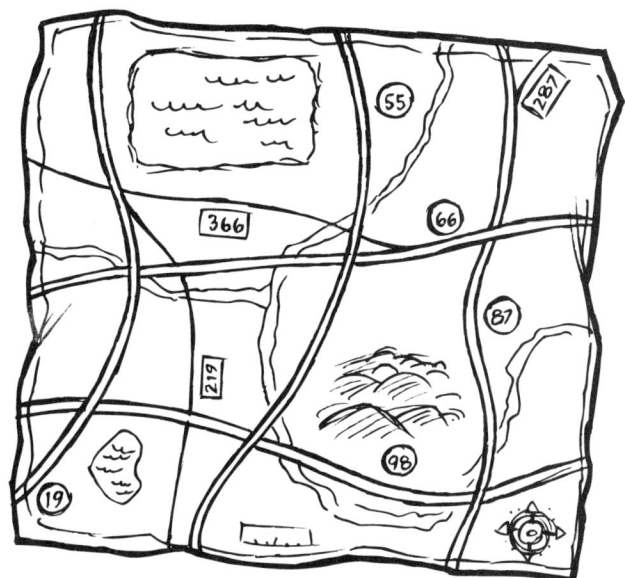

NUMBERS AND COMPUTATION

CONCEPTS FIFTH GRADERS SHOULD KNOW
- place value through billions
- adding and subtracting whole numbers through millions with and without regrouping
- multiplying and dividing with three digit numbers
- adding, subtracting, multiplying, and dividing with decimals to thousandths
- equivalent forms of fractions, decimals, and percents (½ = .50 = 50%)
- comparing and ordering fractions and decimals
- adding and subtracting fractions and mixed numbers with like and unlike denominators
- converting mixed numbers to fractions and fractions to mixed numbers
- estimating and rounding whole numbers, decimals, and fractions

Many students have some confusion about regrouping during whole number subtraction. If the number being subtracted is larger than the number subtracting from, the student needs to "borrow" ten from the next place value. It is often helpful to write the problems with larger numbers and with more space between the digits to allow space for the borrowed digits.

If the student has problems with neatness or keeping columns of numbers lined up properly, provide graph paper of a scale that matches the student's numerals. One numeral should go in each square, except for fractions.

When learning to read and write decimals, ask the student to compare them to their fractional equivalents. When he or she understands that .27 is the same as $^{27}/_{100}$, it will become obvious that to read a decimal number, one need only read the digits as a whole number. For example, the decimal number .104 would have a numerator of 104 when written as a fraction. Three decimal places show to the right of the decimal point. The third place is thousandths. Therefore, the number is read one hundred four thousandths.

An important concept to learn in adding and subtracting decimal numbers is that the places need to line up. The correct answer is found by subtracting hundredths from hundredths, tenths from tenths, and so on. Try to present this idea in many different contexts. For example, it wouldn't make sense to subtract a number of dimes from a number of dollars or a number of crayons from a number of boxes of crayons. This might also be a good time to discuss why 0.49 cents is not equal to $0.49.

When learning to identify fractions, the student should be presented with as many different varieties of problems as possible. In addition to presenting the well-known fractions of a circle, color three out of five stars to show ⅗ or ask the student what part of the chairs at the dining room table are pushed in.

Helpful Hint: Communicate regularly with the child's parent and teacher.

NUMBERS AND COMPUTATION

Students learning new math concepts sometimes prefer to find algorithms (use procedures) that they can apply consistently. While routine is often useful, the mechanical, formulaic approach to math is a major hindrance to mastery and understanding. The observable symptoms of a student relying on algorithms include (1) forgetting one or more steps, (2) going through unnecessary steps in order to complete all steps in the algorithm, and (3) confusing the algorithm for one type of problem with that for another. Two examples of these are performing long division and neglecting to multiply and subtract before bringing down another digit, and multiplying each digit of a factor by 0 or adding 0 to a number.

Another example of relying on the algorithmic approach occurs when changing a mixed number like 3½ to a fraction, 7/2. Students catch on quickly that one need only multiply the denominator and the whole number, then add the numerator. This works every time, but students who do not understand the procedure tend to forget or confuse the steps involved. The use of manipulatives strengthens long-term memory. In the above example, you might cut out three whole circles and a half circle. Give the student a pair of scissors and ask him or her to cut the wholes into halves. Cut out some other wholes and ask the student to do the same. Continue until the student states that he or she doesn't need to cut, since he or she knows that there will be twice as many halves as wholes. Try other mixed numbers the same way.

Activities

1. One of the important math concepts for a fifth grade student to learn is the relationship of place value to multiples of 10. List a number such as 307.45 ten times and ask the student to add the column. Repeat this exercise with other numbers. Help the student recognize that the answer will contain the exact same numerals as the number being added ten times, plus a zero. Write four or five such problems on a page; then show multiplication problems that multiply the same numbers by 10 (for example, 307.45 x 10).

2. Division tells how many of one number there are in another. Demonstrate this by having the student make groups of the same number from a larger number of pieces. Put 147 toothpicks (or other items) on the table. Ask the student to organize them into groups of 7. How many 7s are there? With practice, the student may learn to count out 70 pieces and consider them 10 stacks. When the student discovers this shortcut, write the same division problem on paper and draw connections between what is written and what was modeled.

Helpful Hint: Remind the child of the importance of commas in large numbers.

NUMBERS AND COMPUTATION

3. Most students enjoy play money, and this provides fun opportunities to develop understanding of the decimal system. The student could use play money to subtract large numbers. Make a large number such as 1,307,500 by giving the student one 1 million dollar bill, three 100,000 dollar bills, seven 1 thousand dollar bills, and five 1 hundred dollar bills. Ask the student to subtract a large amount, such as $844,200. The student may borrow by exchanging a bill for ten of the next lowest denomination. Have the student write the answer and say it aloud.

4. There is an effective and fun way to use flash cards. When you present a card, give the student enough time to answer—but not enough time to calculate. This not only encourages memorization and speed, but can be fun. If the student provides the answer quickly and correctly, put the card aside. If the student cannot answer quickly, provide the answer yourself and put the card back into the deck. When the student realizes that you will only let him or her have a second or two, he or she will verbally fumble on those problems that he or she almost knows. This indicates that you are presenting the cards at the right pace.

5. Before practicing addition and subtraction with large numbers, explore the student's understanding of place value. Ask the student to write the largest number that he or she can read correctly. A typical answer is 100,000. Ask for a larger number with the same number of digits. If nothing occurs to the student, ask him or her to add 1 to the number. Ask for an even larger number. The student should realize that the largest possible number with a given number of digits will be written with all nines. Other effective ways to explore place value include working with manipulatives and graph paper. Centimeter cubes can be assembled into sticks of ten, ten sticks can be combined into a sheet of a hundred, and ten sheets may be stacked to make a thousand. This is an effective demonstration of the geometric progression of the decimal system.

6. Many students like to compete against themselves and others. When helping the student learn math facts, record the time it takes him or her to get through the set of flashcards. Review the same cards during following sessions, timing each. Compare the times and ask what the child notices about them. Graphing the time results might motivate the child to beat his or her time. For optimal success, keep the number of flash cards reasonable for the child. If adding the time factor becomes stressful for the student, it may be a sign that he or she needs to review his or her understanding of the concept. Keep this practice fun, not overwhelming!

Helpful Hint: Have all materials ready before the session begins. The student will lose interest if the tutor has to search for supplies.

Name _____ Pretest

Numbers and Computation

Solve. Do not use a calculator.

1) 6,150,487
     +   340,498

2) 28) 14,084

3) $13 \frac{7}{16}$
     $- 7 \frac{3}{16}$

4) 507
     × 48

5) What fraction is shown?

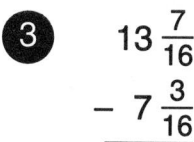

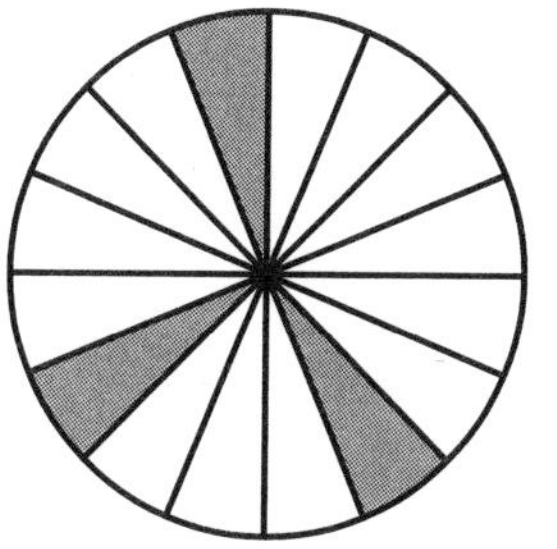

_____

6) Arrange in order from least to greatest:

$\frac{3}{8}, \frac{1}{3}, \frac{5}{12}$ _____

7) Add. Express your answer as a fraction in lowest terms.

$2\frac{3}{4} + \frac{3}{4}$ _____

8) Write two fractions that are equal to $\frac{3}{4}$.

_____   _____

© 2001 Frank Schaffer Publications, Inc.   FS122133 The Tutor's Handbook: Math Grade 5

 Name _____

Numbers and Computation

Using Decimals

Solve.

1) 12.043
   − 7.548

2) .28) .756

3) 6.028
   + .833

4) 3.08
   × 10

5) Write the number two hundred and twenty thousandths in numeric form.
_____

6) Round 0.178 to the nearest hundredth. _____

7) Change 0.45 into a fraction. _____

8) Fernando kept a record of his sleep. He found that on average, he slept 60.5 hours per week. At this rate, how many hours would he sleep in a year?

_____ hours

© 2001 Frank Schaffer Publications, Inc.

FS122133 The Tutor's Handbook: Math Grade 5

Using Fractions

1 Write in simplest form.

$\frac{24}{28}$ _____

2 Change to a mixed number.

$\frac{27}{14}$ _____

3 8 inches is what part of a foot? _____

4 Arrange in order from least to greatest.

$\frac{3}{4}$ $\frac{3}{6}$ $\frac{1}{3}$

_____

Add.

5 $\frac{7}{10} + \frac{2}{10} =$

6 $\frac{1}{3} + \frac{3}{4} =$

Subtract.

7 $3\frac{4}{5} - 1\frac{2}{5} =$

8 $\frac{6}{8} - \frac{1}{2} =$

9 Change $\frac{1}{4}$ into a decimal.

_____

Posttest

Numbers and Computation

Solve. Do not use a calculator.

1) 25.368
 +12.017

2) 8.2 − .7 =

3) 609
 × 57

4) 42) 25,368

5) $6\frac{5}{6}$ + _____ = $8\frac{2}{3}$

6) 7,060,250
 − 2,060,274

7) $\frac{5}{8} + \frac{2}{3}$ =

8) What number is 409,108 more than 527,374?

 _____

9) Circle the largest number.

 $\frac{26}{6}$, $\frac{45}{10}$, $4\frac{1}{3}$

10) Circle the fraction that equals 0.416.

 $\frac{5}{12}$ $\frac{1}{5}$ $\frac{3}{8}$

11) Round 4,307.805 to the nearest hundredth.

 _____

© 2001 Frank Schaffer Publications, Inc.

FS122133 The Tutor's Handbook: Math Grade 5

PATTERNS

> **CONCEPTS FIFTH GRADERS SHOULD KNOW**
> - identifying, describing, and extending geometric and numeric patterns
> - using patterns to predict outcomes
> - identifying and describing patterns using tables and graphs
> - relationships between quantities that aid problem solving

Listen carefully to the student's description of a pattern. Typically, a student will first come up with a description that sounds almost right but that is not wholly accurate. For example, if the pattern is triangle, square, pentagon, and so on, the student might notice that the shapes are getting bigger (taking up more surface area). It is more accurate to say that the number of sides is increasing. Developing this mathematical vocabulary and accurate thinking is a principal objective of this section.

Number Sequences

The easiest number sequence to recognize is basic skip counting (2, 4, 6, 8, 10).

Another easily recognized number sequence is one in which the same number is added each time to get the next number, as in 3, 10, 17, 24, 31... (adding seven).

It is more difficult to recognize an addition sequence in which a pattern of two or more numbers are added in turn. For example, in the following sequence, 3 and 5 are alternately added: 4, 7, 12, 15, 20, 23, 28.

There are many naturally occurring patterns in which the number being added increases by one each time. Thus 1 is added to the first number to make the second, 2 is added to the second to make the third, and so on (1, 2, 4, 7, 11 . . .).

Some sequences can be seen as direct variations—that is, the position of a number in the sequence times a consistent factor determines the value of the number. If the factor is 6, then the third number in the sequence will be 18. Such a sequence can also be seen as addition but it is helpful to establish the multiplication function when the task is to predict the value of a number in the sequence. For example, what would be the 25th number in the sequence given in the box below?

> **Helpful Hint:** Patterns can often be described in more than one way. If the student describes a pattern in a way that has not occurred to you, help him or her learn to check the pattern's consistency.

1.5, 3, 4.5, 6, 7.5, 9, 10.5 . . .		position in sequence	25
	x	factor	x 1.5
		number in sequence	37.5

PATTERNS

Geometric Shapes

In a geometric sequence, each shape is changed in the same way. The shape may be rotated the same number of degrees each time. The shaded part of a shape may rotate clockwise. A sequence of polygons may each have one more side than the one before (triangle, square, pentagon, hexagon, and so on). Groups of shapes may change relative position: a circle, square, and triangle may be followed by a triangle, circle, square, then by a square, triangle, and circle, and so on.

Using Tables, Graphs, and Pictures

When the student is unsure about how to solve a problem, he or she can always try "guess and check." If guesses or possible solutions are organized with a table, a pattern will usually emerge that makes the solution easier to find. Sometimes it is not obvious to the student how to go about setting up a table or graph. Help him or her understand how to use a table and determine appropriate column headings. In the following sample problem, the student's guesses are listed in a table. By comparing the results, the student knows whether guesses are too high or too low.

To use this table, the student guesses a number of dimes. The number of nickels is double the number of dimes. The values are calculated from the number of each type of coin. The total of the values is to equal $1.80. In the table below, it is obvious that the guesses of 5 and 7 are too low. A higher guess is made, which turns out to be too high. In this way, guesses can be narrowed until the answer is found.

Discussion after a problem is solved is important for a student learning to recognize patterns. Often a pattern will appear that was not recognized before. This unrecognized pattern would likely have made the problem easier to solve. In the table below, it is easy to see that the values of the dimes and nickels are always equal. Ask the student why this is. Discuss with him or her how this discovery might be used to help solve future problems.

Rebecca has $1.80 in nickels and dimes. She has twice as many nickels as dimes. How many nickels and how many dimes does she have?

Build a table that shows the relationships provided in the problem. The number of nickels depends on the number of dimes, and the total value depends on the number of nickels and dimes.

Dimes	Nickels	Value of Dimes	Value of Nickels	Total Value
5	10	$ .50	$ .50	$1.00
7	14	$ .70	$ .70	$1.40
12	24	$1.20	$ 1.20	$2.40
10	20	$1.00	$ 1.00	$2.00
9	18	$ .90	$ .90	$1.80

PATTERNS

Activities

1. Practice with different types of number sequences. Provide the student with sequences such as a number being repeated, a number being added, a number being multiplied, and a number being subtracted. Label each type of sequence until the student is able to figure it out on his or her own. If the child masters these, practice determining a number further along the sequence.

2. Making a graph of numbers in a pattern will reveal a visual representation of the pattern. Have the child make a simple bar graph using the numbers in the sequence. He or she will soon see the pattern emerge.

Helpful Hint:
Make sure the child feels successful before challenging him or her to more difficult items.

3. To help the student understand sequences of geometric shapes, cut out some shapes from colored construction paper and ask the student to experiment with putting them together in different ways. Encourage him or her to try rotating each of the shapes in turn. Let the student create his or her own patterns by adding a shape each time or by rotating one or more of the shapes.

4. Make a pattern with everyday objects. Bring a shoebox filled with various household objects to the session such as buttons, paperclips, rubber bands, and crayons. Make sure that you provide enough of each object to create a pattern. Encourage the student to create patterns with the objects. After he or she designs a pattern, ask the student to describe the pattern in writing.

5. Provide the student with a piece of graph paper and colored pencils. Ask him or her to color a pattern on the graph paper. Encourage the student to experiment with many different types of patterns. Have him or her write out an explanation for each pattern to demonstrate complete understanding.

6. To help the student accurately identify and state a pattern, design three patterns. After the student has had a chance to examine them, read a description of one of the patterns and ask the student to indicate which pattern you described. Extend this activity and use objects in the child's environment. For example, ask the child to describe a pattern found in the cereal aisle of the grocery store.

_____ Pretest

Name

Patterns

1 Draw the next shape in this series.

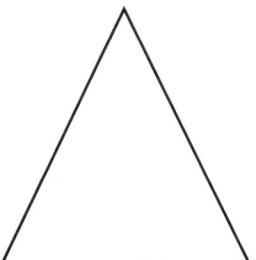  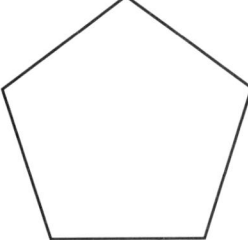

2 Find the next number in this sequence. _____

4, 19, 34, 49 . . .

3 What number goes in the blank?

| 5,000 | 2,500 | 1,250 | 625 | 312.50 |
| 500 | 250 | 125 | 62.50 | _____ |

4 How many Xs will there be in the seventh row in this pattern? _____

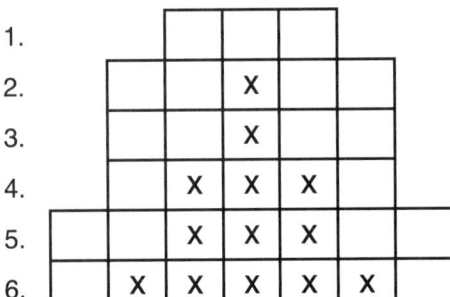

5 What will the fifteenth character in this sequence be? _____

a, b, c, 9, d, e, f, 18, g, h, i, 27, . . .

Name ______________________________

Number Patterns

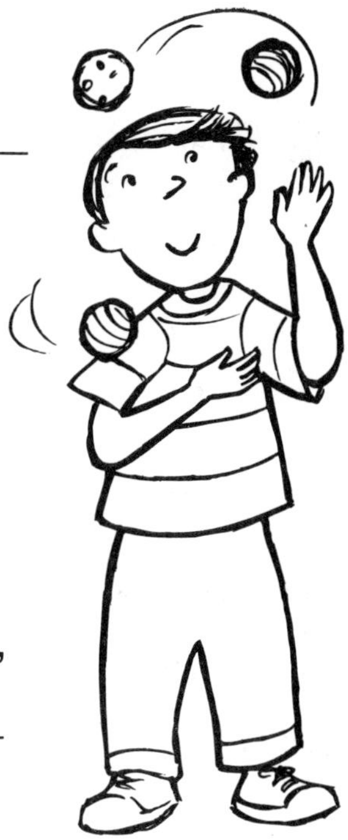

1. Find the next two letter pairs in this sequence. ________, ________

   AB, AC, AD, BC, BD, BE, CD, CE, . . .

2. What will be the last number in this pattern? __________

1		2		3		4		4		3		2		1
	3		5		7		8		7		5		3	
		8		12		15		15		12		8		
			20		27		30		27		20			

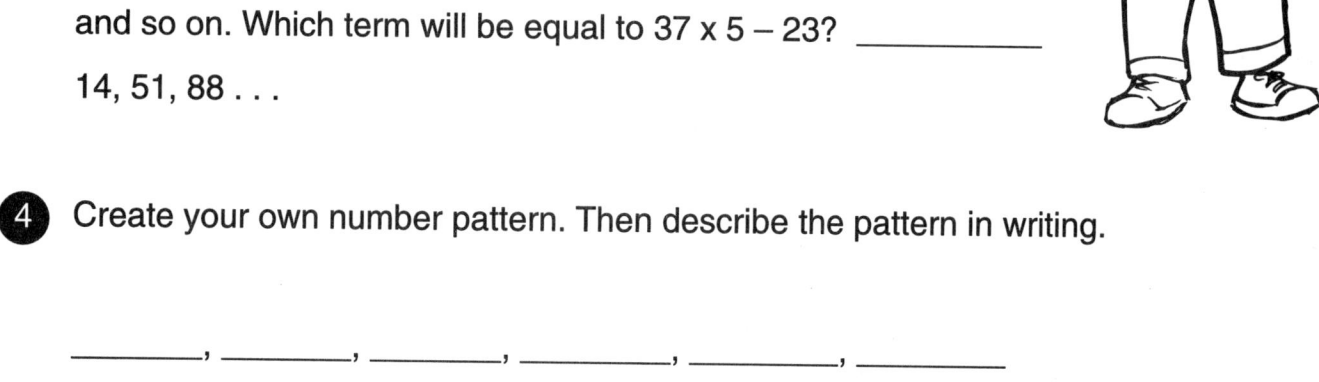

3. In the sequence below, the first term is 14, the second term is 51, and so on. Which term will be equal to 37 x 5 – 23? __________

   14, 51, 88 . . .

4. Create your own number pattern. Then describe the pattern in writing.

   ________, ________, ________, ________, ________, ________

   ____

   ____

5. Create your own pattern using shapes and colors. Then describe the pattern in writing.

   ____

   ____

   ____

 Name _____   Patterns

Predictable Patterns

1 Mr. and Mrs. Hernandez went out to dinner with their friends, Mr. and Mrs. Jackson. The waiter took their orders. Two people ordered pasta, one person ordered fish, and the other person ordered beef. Unfortunately, the waiter forgot who ordered what. How many possible arrangements are there for these meals?

_____ possible arrangements

2 What number goes in the blank?

$300 divided 4 ways = $75.00 each

$600 divided 8 ways = $75.00 each

$900 divided 12 ways = $75.00 each

$1,200 divided _____ ways = $75.00 each

3 How many three-letter words with letters in alphabetical order can be made with the letters a, b, c, d, e, f, and g? (No proper nouns, no letters repeated.)

_____ words

4 What would be the 40th number in this sequence? _____

7, 12, 17, 22, 27 . . .

© 2001 Frank Schaffer Publications, Inc. FS122133 The Tutor's Handbook: Math Grade 5

 Name _____ Patterns

Patterns Practice

1 How many three-digit multiples of 7 are even numbers?

_____

2 State a rule. What is happening to the starting number each time? Finish the table.

_____
_____
_____

Starting Number	Ending Number
2	5
10	25
14	35
16	40
20	____
32	____

3 Find 5 three-digit multiples of 19 that are palindromes (they read the same way backward as forward). Their first digits are 1, 3, 4, 6, and 9.

_____
_____
_____
_____
_____

© 2001 Frank Schaffer Publications, Inc.   25 reproducible   FS122133 The Tutor's Handbook: Math Grade 5

Name _____   Posttest

Patterns

1 If this pattern is continued until there are forty shapes in all, what fraction of the shapes will have dots in them? _____

2 What are the next 2 numbers in this sequence?

14, 31, 48, 65, _____, _____

3 How many triangles are in this design? _____

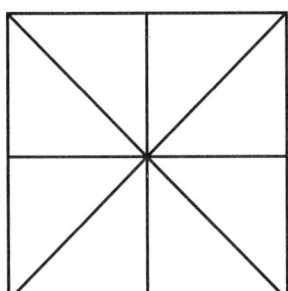

4 The 203rd multiple of 7 will have what numeral in the ones place? _____

5 If the pattern below is continued, how many blank squares will be in the first figure that contains the number 32? _____

Geometry

CONCEPTS FIFTH GRADERS SHOULD KNOW
- identifying, describing and classifying two- and three-dimensional shapes: **triangles, circles, quadrilaterals, polygons, prisms, pyramid, cone, cylinder, and sphere**
- **identifying the line of symmetry**
- **identifying or predicting the results of flips, slides, and turns**
- **using ordered pairs on a coordinate grid**
- **geometric vocabulary**

Most students enjoy geometry because it is visual and much of the learning is hands on. When teaching geometry concepts, use visual models whenever possible, especially when discussing three-dimensional shapes. The concept of representing three-dimensional shapes on two-dimensional paper is difficult for fifth grade students students to grasp. Ask the student to describe what he or she sees—don't assume that he or she recognizes the depth of a three-dimensional drawing. Whenever possible, ask the student to explain what he or she is doing and to explain his or her conclusions. Help the student use geometric vocabulary to accurately describe what he or she sees.

Helpful Hint: Visit your local teacher supply store and purchase sets of cubes, prisms, geoboards, and other aids that make geometry more fun!

The student may need instruction on how to identify polygons. Remind him or her that polygons are named for the number of sides the shape has. For example, a quadrilateral has four sides.

When helping the student with congruent shapes, remind him or her that congruent shapes have the same shape and size. However, many congruent shapes do not present themselves in the same way. Sometimes the shapes may be turned, flipped, or slid. Challenge the student to find congruent shapes in the room in which he or she is working.

The line of symmetry divides a shape so that both parts of the shape are exactly the same. Suggest drawing a shape on a piece of paper and folding it in half. When the paper is unfolded, does the fold show congruent shapes on either side? If so, that is the line of symmetry.

The student should always label answers with the correct units. The concept of one, two, and three dimensions is not apparent to students of this age, and it is best to establish the connection between linear units (as in a pencil line one centimeter long), square units (as in a 1 cm x 1 cm square on graph paper), and cubic units (as in the solid cubes used to demonstrate volume).

Two-dimensional shapes may also be explored with coordinate graphing. The activities that follow only use the positive coordinates in the first quadrant; however, when you draw a graph to work on coordinates with the student, draw it so that part of the other quadrants show. A curious student will sometimes ask what numbers would be "out there." Rather than answering directly, ask leading questions to encourage the student to explore what those other numbers mean. Remind the student to move horizontally and then vertically on the coordinate grid. Give the student several inverse pairs of coordinates, such as (3,2) and (2,3), to emphasize the difference.

   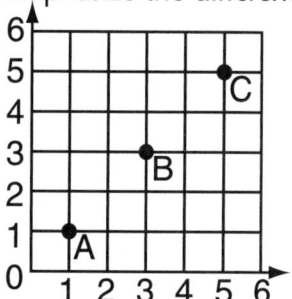

GEOMETRY

Activities

1. Help the student learn geometric terms. Have him or her create a geometry dictionary. Terms and drawings to include: *point, line, line segment, ray, plane, angle, right angle, acute angle, obtuse angle, congruent, intersecting lines, perpendicular lines, parallel lines, vertex, edge, face, chord, diameter, radius, circle, semicircle, square, quadrilateral, parallelogram, rhombus, rectangle, equilateral triangle, isosceles triangle, scalene triangle, right triangle*. Most definitions can be found in the glossary of the student's math textbook. Check with the child's teacher to see if there are any other terms the student needs for the classroom. Once the student has learned the geometry vocabulary, encourage its use as often as possible.

2. Reinforce coordinate graphing with a game. Play tic-tac-toe on a coordinate graph. Four Xs or Os in a horizontal, vertical, or diagonal row win. Each player must name the coordinate before marking it.

3. Another effective way to teach vocabulary and names of the geometric shapes is to write the word or draw the shape on one side of an index card and the definition or name of the shape on the other side. When showing the student the flash cards, have him or her work through them quickly. If the student cannot provide an answer immediately, show him or her the answer; then return the card to the back of the deck. If an answer is given quickly and correctly, set the card aside.

4. Make learning about the line of symmetry a fun art project! Ask the student to fold a large piece of white paper in half so that there is a vertical line in the middle of the paper. Next, ask the student to paint a simple design on the left side of the paper. While the paint is still wet, help the child carefully fold the paper on the line, flattening the two sides together. Ask the student to open the paper to find that the design has mirrored itself on the right side of the paper. Discuss the new design. Help him or her realize that the right side is a mirror image of the left. Extend this activity by drawing some geometric shapes onto a piece of paper. Encourage the student to find the line of symmetry in each shape.

5. Provide the student with some real life experiences with three dimensional solids. Bring in some examples of solids such as an ice cream cone (cone), a soda can (cylinder) a tennis ball (sphere), a rectangular box (rectangular prism), and a die (cube). Encourage the student to thoroughly explore each object. Pose questions that require the student to examine the faces, edges, and vertices. Discuss what makes each object unique.

6. Flips, slides, and turns are physical motions encountered when common objects are moved. Practice each of these concepts by cutting two congruent triangles out of an index card. Place the two triangles on top of each other on the table. Move one of the triangles and ask the child to identify what the move shows: flip, slide, or turn. Try this using various objects to practice flipping, sliding and turning.

Helpful Hint: A flip is to move a figure over a line so that the figure faces in the opposite direction. A slide is to move a figure along a straight line without changing direction. A turn is to move a figure along a curved path around a point either clockwise or counterclockwise.

 _____ Pretest

Geometry

Write the name of each shape.

1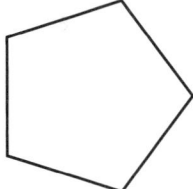

2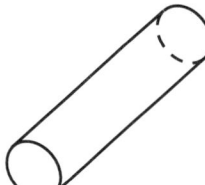

3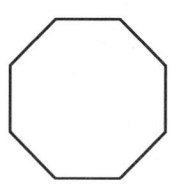

_____   _____   _____

4 Draw a line of symmetry through each shape.

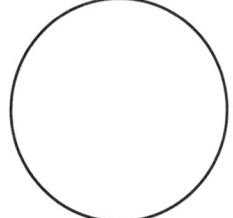   

Use the coordinate grid to answer the questions.

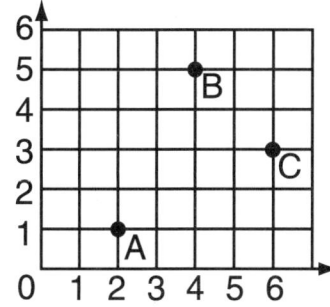

5 What letter is at point (6,3)? _____

6 On what point is the letter B? _____

7 What letter is at point (2,1)? _____

© 2001 Frank Schaffer Publications, Inc.　　　FS122133 The Tutor's Handbook: Math Grade 5

 Name _____   Geometry

Shapes and Symmetry

Match the names on the left with their corresponding objects on the right.

_____ ① Cylinder

_____ ② Cone

_____ ③ Sphere

_____ ④ Rectangular prism

a.

b.

c.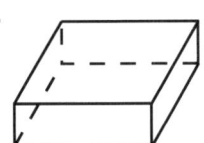

d.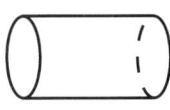

Write the name of each space figure.

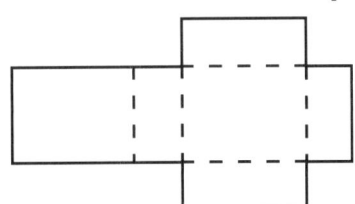

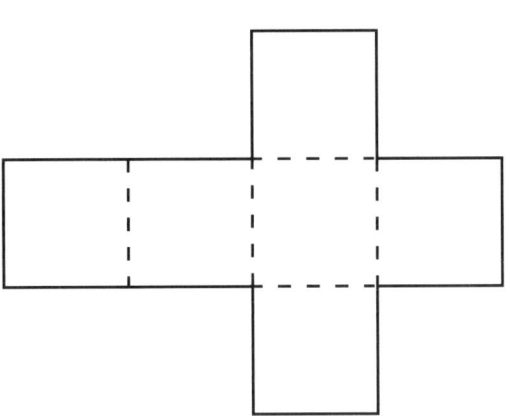

⑤ _____

⑥ _____

Draw the line of symmetry through each shape.

⑦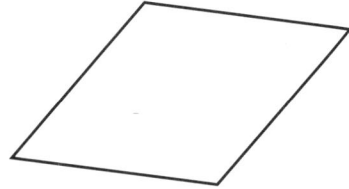

⑧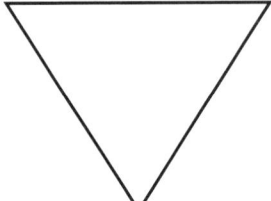

© 2001 Frank Schaffer Publications, Inc.   30 reproducible   FS122133 The Tutor's Handbook: Math Grade 5

 Name _____ Geometry

Coordinate Graphing

Use the graph at right to answer questions 1 through 4.

1. Give the coordinates of the location halfway between points B and E.

   (____,____)

2. Between which two points could you travel by going an equal number across and up or down?

   ____ and ____

3. Give the coordinates of the location 3 points to the left of point A.

   (____,____)

4. Find the area of the triangle made by connecting points F, C, and E. What is the area of the triangle?

   _____

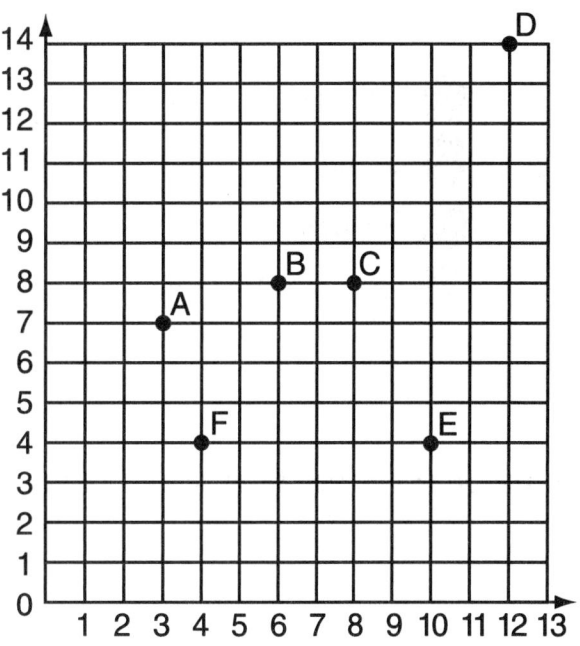

Use the graph below to answer questions 5 and 6.

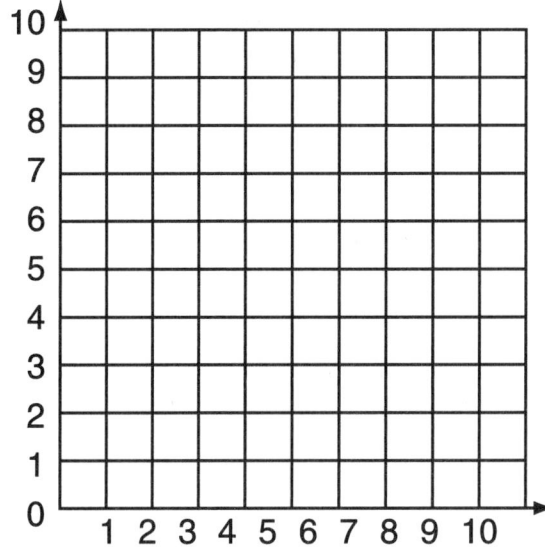

Plot the following points in the order given: (2,9), (9,9), (9,7), (8,7), (8,6), (9,6) (9,1), (6,1), (6,5), (4,5), (4,3), and (2,3).

5. What is the perimeter of this figure?

   _____

6. What is the area of the figure?

   _____

© 2001 Frank Schaffer Publications, Inc.   31 reproducible   FS122133 The Tutor's Handbook: Math Grade 5

 _____ Geometry

Congruent Figures

Congruent figures are the same shape and size.

Circle the shape that is congruent to the one shown.

 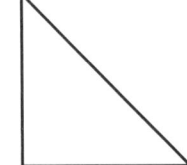   a. 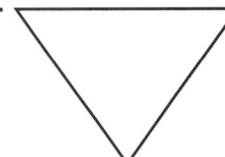   b. 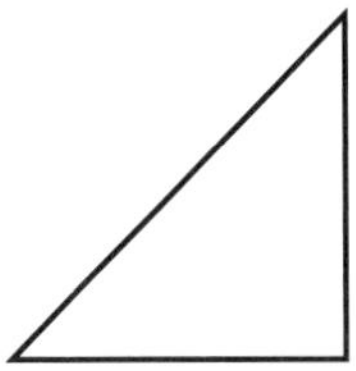 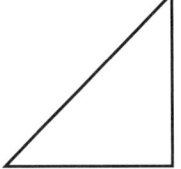   c.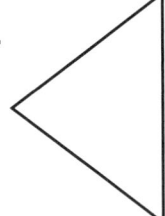

② 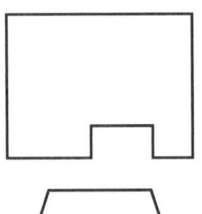   a. 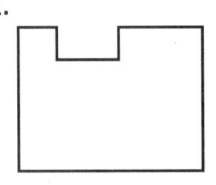   b. 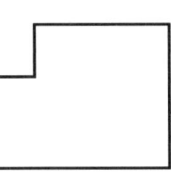   c.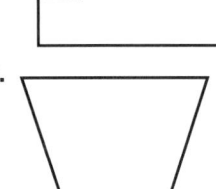

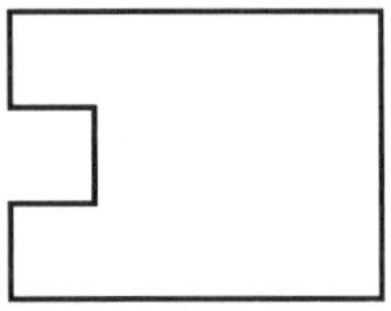

③ (trapezoid)   a. 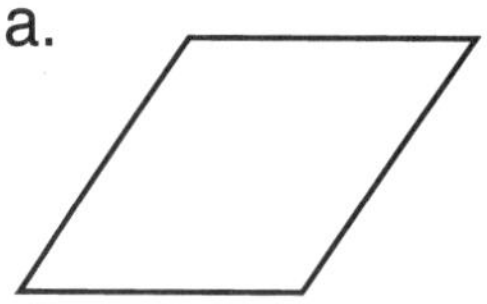 (parallelogram)   b. 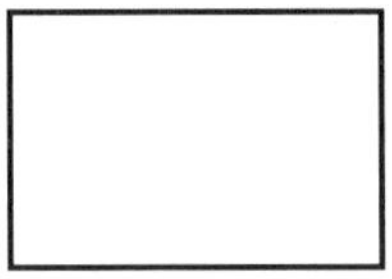 (rectangle)   c. (trapezoid)

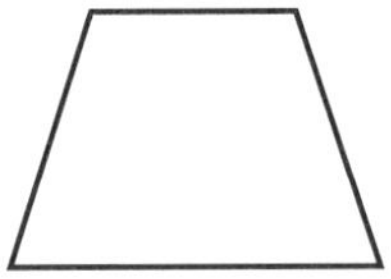

Determine how each shape has been moved. Write *flip*, *slide*, or *turn*.

④    ⑤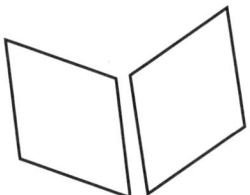

_____   _____

⑥    ⑦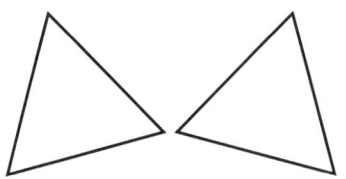

_____   _____

© 2001 Frank Schaffer Publications, Inc.   32   FS122133 The Tutor's Handbook: Math Grade 5

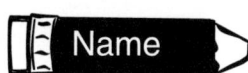 _____ Posttest

Geometry

Write the name of each shape.

1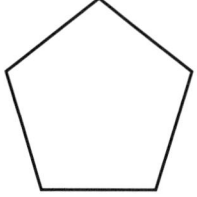

_____

2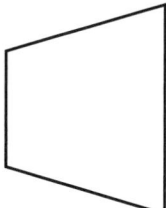

_____

3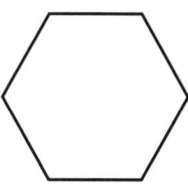

_____

4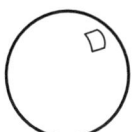

_____

5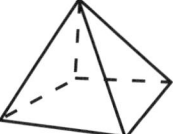

_____

6

_____

Plot the points on the grid. Mark each point with the letter.

7 A (3,2)
   B (1,4)
   C (5,6)
   D (6,5)
   E (8,7)

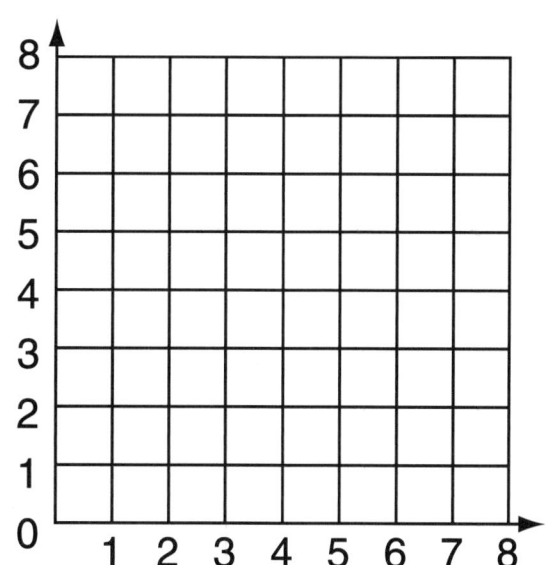

© 2001 Frank Schaffer Publications, Inc.   33 reproducible   FS122133 The Tutor's Handbook: Math Grade 5

MEASUREMENT

CONCEPTS FIFTH GRADERS SHOULD KNOW
- measurements in U.S. customary and metric systems
- identifying and applying correct U.S. customary or metric units of measurement
- estimating measurements
- conversions within a system of measurement
- area, perimeter, and volume of shapes

Getting to Know the Units of Measurement

The basic units of the metric system are meters (distance), grams (mass and weight), and liters (capacity). The units of metric measure are decimal, and their relative sizes are indicated by prefixes such as *kilo-* (1000), *hecto-* (100), *deka-* (10), *deci-* (1/10), *centi-* (1/100), *milli-* (1/1,000), and *micro-* (1/1,000,000). Thus a hectogram would be 100 grams, a kiloliter 1,000 liters, a centimeter 1/100 meter, and so on. Students need to memorize the prefixes and know the decimal value of each.

Metric	U.S. Customary
length	length
1 centimeter = 10 millimeters	1 foot = 12 inches
1 decimeter = 10 centimeters	1 yard = 3 feet
1 meter = 10 decimeters	1 mile = 5,280 feet
mass/weight	mass/weight
1 kilogram = 1,000 grams	1 pound = 16 ounces
	1 ton = 2,000 pounds
capacity	capacity
1 liter = 1,000 milliliters	1 cup = 8 fluid ounces
	1 pint = 2 cups
	1 quart = 2 pints
	1 gallon = 4 quarts

MEASUREMENT

Measuring

Measuring customary units requires a good understanding of fractions, and measuring in the metric system requires a good understanding of decimals.

Students can have difficulty reading fractions of inches marked on a ruler. Start by drawing lines and asking the student to find their lengths. After the student is able to do this, ask him or her to make a line 1¼ inches longer.

A metric ruler usually labels centimeters. Between each centimeter are ten markings for millimeters. If the student measures a line and finds it halfway between 7 and 8 centimeters, he or she should know that the line is either 7.5 cm or 75 mm.

Converting Units

Because we ordinarily only use one measurement system or the other, little emphasis is placed on converting units from customary to metric or vice versa. It is necessary, however, to be able to convert units within each system.

To convert from one unit to another in the customary system, the student must know all of the equivalents: 16 ounces to a pound, 5,280 feet to a mile, and so on. It is helpful to demonstrate these with rulers and weights. Identify each unit with something that the student knows. Does the math text weigh two pounds? How far does the student live from school?

Converting customary units usually puts the metric system in a favorable light. When converting from one metric unit to another, only the decimal point and unit prefix change; the numerals stay the same (plus or minus zeroes). The basic metric units of mass and capacity, the gram and the liter, are both based upon metric units of distance. A gram is the weight of a cubic centimeter of water. A liter is the capacity of a cubic decimeter of water. So 100 cm^3 = 100 grams = 100 ml.

Combining Units

Adding and subtracting customary units often involves conversion. After finding a sum, the student is expected to rewrite the answer in simplest form. A sum of 1 foot 15 inches should be changed to 2 feet 3 inches. When subtracting, the student will need to borrow and change the borrowed unit into the appropriate number of units being used. For example, if time is being subtracted and it is necessary to borrow from the hours, 60 should be added to the number of minutes.

> **Helpful Hint:**
> Make learning about measurement a fun, realistic experience. Help the child discover all the uses of measurement in daily life: measuring ingredients in cooking, the distance from home to school, or the time spent on homework.

MEASUREMENT

Activities

1. Make a list of words that have the same or similar prefixes as metric prefixes. How many words can the student think of that have *cent* in them (meaning 100 or 1/100)? The student may know the words *percent* and *century*. Help the child discover other measurement words such as *decade* and *millennium*.

2. Have the student estimate the heights of his or her brothers, sisters, or parents in both customary and metric units. Then have the student check the estimates by actually measuring the heights of the family members with a measuring tape. If there is a large discrepancy between the estimates and the actual measurements, have the student estimate and measure the lengths of more objects until his or her estimates are more accurate. The student can estimate and measure just about any object!

3. The marks indicating fractional units on a ruler are small and sometimes hard to read. Provide a large, long piece of paper or a long, flat stick and have the student draw an oversize ruler. Not only will the differences between the fourths and the eighths marks show up better, but making the giant ruler will strengthen the student's measuring skills. If the student wanted to make the giant ruler three feet long and have it represent one foot, how would he or she measure and draw the units? Explore similar questions with the student. Choose a scale that not only fits the paper, but that will be easy to work with.

4. Help the student develop a sense of various weights. Provide sinkers from your local fishing tackle store. Each weight is clearly marked in ounces. Have the student use a balance scale to make comparisons. How many two ounce weights equal one pound?

5. An effective way to practice converting customary units is to use measuring cups and pitchers. Fill a large container with water. How many cups does it take to fill a quart container? Point out the pint marks on the pitcher. If none are present, make some with a felt tip pen or tape. How many pints can be filled with the quart container? If one pint and one cup were removed from the quart container, how much water would be left? Use a metric measuring cup to practice with the metric system.

6. It is interesting for the student to explore the relationship of perimeter and area. Use a pre-measured length of wire or other stiff material. Have the student determine the perimeter by measuring it. Ask the student to form it into a

> **Helpful Hint:**
> Area = length x width
> Perimeter = sum of all the sides
> Volume = length x width x height

rectangle. Have him or her determine the length and width of the rectangle made and then calculate the area. Ask the student to form the wire into another rectangle and again record the dimensions and the area. Have the student make as many different rectangles as possible. Which rectangle has the greatest area? Why is that?

Name _____ Pretest

Measurement

1) 45 cm = _____ m

2) 5 feet = _____ yards

3) Find the perimeter of the triangle.

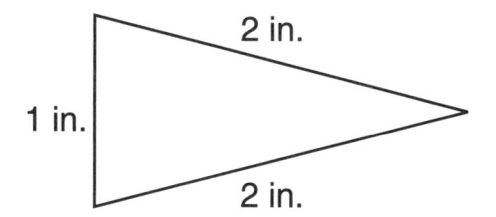

- 2 in.
- 1 in.
- 2 in.

_____ inches

4) Which of these weighs more than you?

a. 1000 grams

b. $\frac{1}{4}$ ton

c. 100 ounces

d. 5,000,000 milligrams

5) Find the area of this shape.

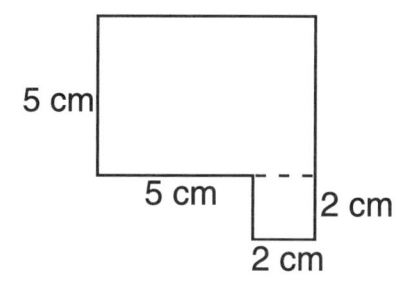

- 5 cm
- 5 cm
- 2 cm
- 2 cm

_____ sq. cm

6) Find the volume of the rectangular prism.

- 7 cm
- 8 cm
- 6 cm

_____ cm³

7) It takes Albert 1 hour and 20 minutes to drive from his house to the town of Cedarville. If he leaves home at 11:15 a.m., when will he arrive? _____

8) Find the perimeter of a rectangle that measures $5\frac{1}{4}$ inches by $3\frac{3}{4}$ inches. _____

9) Find the area of a rectangle that measures $11\frac{1}{2}$ inches by $4\frac{1}{2}$ inches. _____

Name _____ Measurement

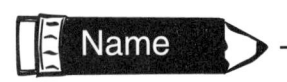

Metric Measurement

kilo-	hecto-	deka-	unit	deci-	centi-	milli-
1,000	100	10	1	.1	.01	.001

Convert each measurement.

1. 5 kilometers = _____ meters
2. 10 decimeters = _____ meter
3. 2 dekameters = _____ meters
4. 300 centimeters = _____ meters

5. 8 kilometers = _____ hectometers
6. 25 centimeters = _____ decimeters
7. 8 dekameters = _____ centimeters
8. 0.1 kilometer = _____ meters

Increase each of the following by 2.5 centiliters.

9. 28.2 centiliters

10. 5.25 liters

11. 50 milliliters

_____ centiliters   _____ liters   _____ milliliters

12. Find the perimeter of this rectangle.

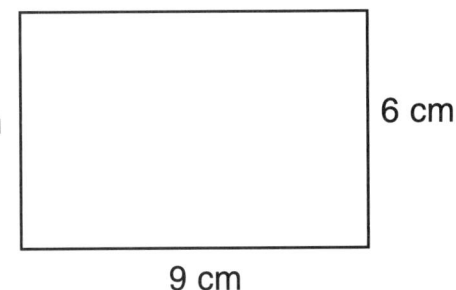

    _____

    9 cm
    6 cm   6 cm
    9 cm

13. Measure the line below and express your answer in millimeters, centimeters, decimeters, and meters.

    _____

    _____ mm   _____ cm   _____ dm   _____ m

Name _____

Measurement

U.S. Customary Units

Solve each problem.

1. During the big storm, the height of the river started at 4 feet 8 inches and rose 3 inches per hour for the next 15 hours. How high did the river get? _____

2. If a yardstick were divided into four equal pieces, how long would each piece be? Express your answer as a fraction of a foot. _____

3. Divide the figure at the right into two rectangles and then find the total area.
   _____

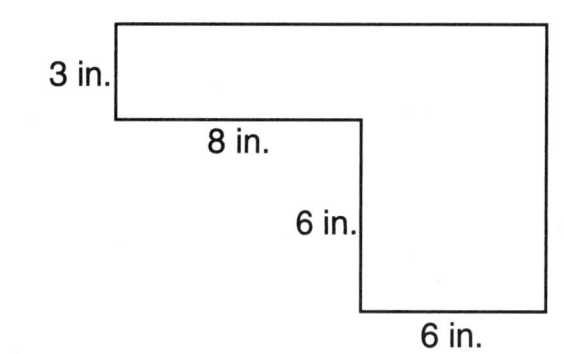

   3 in.
   8 in.
   6 in.
   6 in.

4. Subtract.
   4 yards 1 foot 8 inches – 2 yards 10 inches
   _____

5. Wen walks at 5 m.p.h. How long does it take him to walk 8 miles? Express your answer in hours and minutes. _____

6. At 9:00 a.m., Leila began walking west at 4 m.p.h. At 10:00 a.m., Deshawn left from the same place and began walking towards Leila in hopes of catching up with her. If Deshawn walked a mile every 12 minutes, when would he catch up with Leila?
   _____

	Leila	Deshawn
10:00	4 mi	0 mi
11:00		
12:00		
1:00		

© 2001 Frank Schaffer Publications, Inc.　　　39　　　FS122133 The Tutor's Handbook: Math Grade 5
reproducible

Other U.S. Customary Units

Solve each problem.

1 2,000 minutes = _____ hours

2 Which is longer, 1,000 days or 2 years 8 months?

_____

3 50 tons = _____ pounds

4 Water weighs about one pound per pint. There are 8 pints in a gallon. How many gallons are in a ton of water?

_____

5 Susan started her homework at 3:40 p.m. She finished at 5:10. How long did it take Susan to do her homework?

_____

6 $2\frac{1}{2}$ cups = _____ pints

7 If all of the outside cubes were removed from the rectangular prism below, what would be the volume of the smaller cube that would remain?

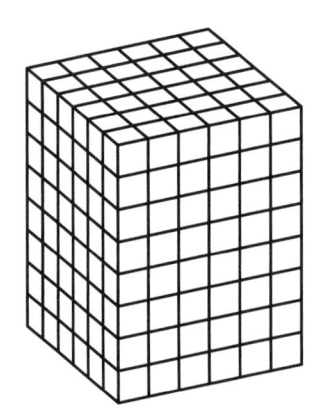

_____

Name _____   Posttest

Measurement

1 Which distance would take the longest amount of time to walk?

a. 5 meters   c. 3000 cm

b. 4,000 mm   d. 4000 hm

2 6.8 hm = _____ m

3 180 inches = _____ yards

4 What is the area of the figure to the right?
_____

5 What is the perimeter of the figure to the right?
_____

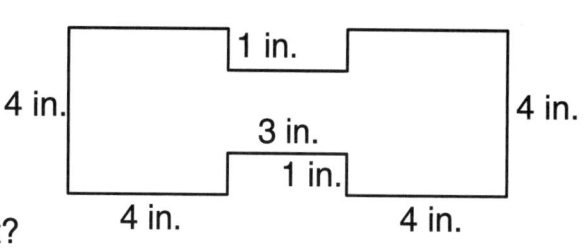

(Figure labels: 1 in., 4 in., 3 in., 1 in., 4 in., 4 in., 4 in., 4 in.)

6 Find the volume of this rectangular prism.
_____

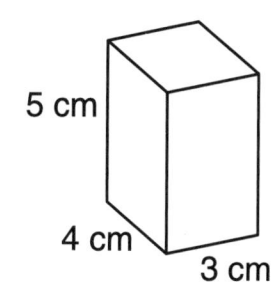

(Prism labels: 5 cm, 4 cm, 3 cm)

7 Cynthia started her art project at 3:30 p.m. and finished it 2 hours and 45 minutes later. What time was it when she finished? _____

DATA ANALYSIS, STATISTICS, AND PROBABILITY

CONCEPTS FIFTH GRADERS SHOULD KNOW
- collecting and organizing data
- creating and interpreting tables and graphs: bar graphs, line graphs, circle graphs, and pictographs
- finding averages
- making predictions based on data
- determining the probability of an event and describing it as *certain*, *equally likely*, or *impossible*
- representing the likelihood of an event as a number between 0 and 1

Organizing Data

As data usually occurs in unorganized lists, the first task is to reorder the data, by group if appropriate. If there are several instances of the same score, it may be simpler to make tallies or list the scores in rows. Tell the student to count all of the tallied scores afterward to be sure that none have been inadvertently left out.

Graphs and Tables

The student should have some experience with graphs and tables but will probably need help selecting the type of graph or table to use with a particular set of data. If there is a mathematical or causal relationship between two conditions, a line graph may be best. If there is no definite mathematical relationship, a bar graph may be better. For example, if a student wanted to graph the growth of a bean plant grown in science class, a line graph would show the height of the plant relative to the number of days passed. If the student wanted to show the results of a survey of students' favorite TV shows, a bar graph would be appropriate.

Helpful Hint: Vary the orientation of graphs. The student should be familiar with both horizontal and vertical graphs.

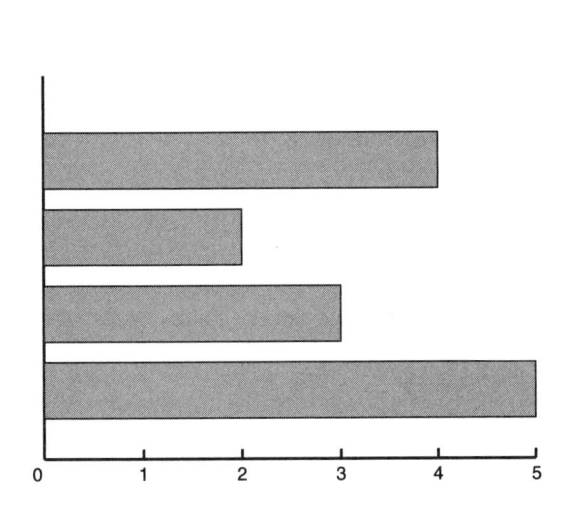

Bar graph

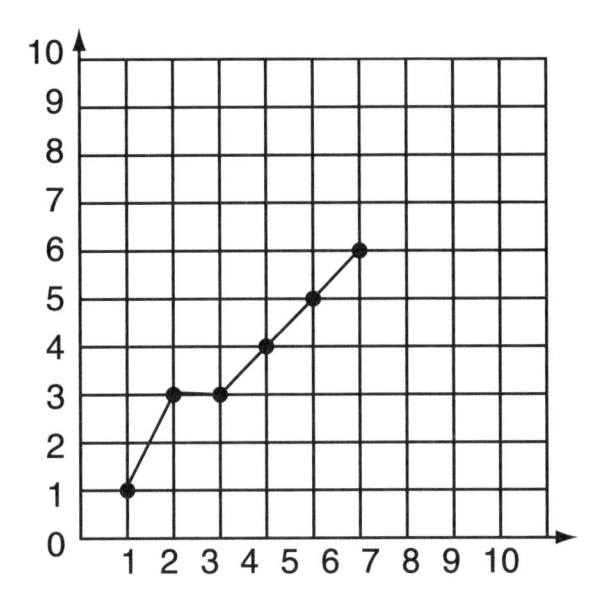

Line graph

42

DATA ANALYSIS, STATISTICS, AND PROBABILITY

Probability

Probability is usually expressed as a fraction, with the numerator reflecting a specific outcome and the denominator representing the total number of possible outcomes. The probability of getting a four when rolling one die is $1/6$. The probability of getting an even number is $3/6$.

Probability is a new concept to students at this level. You may be tempted to introduce probability calculations, but it is better for now to teach the student the language of probability and help him or her understand what probability is. If the probability of an event is $5/6$, how many times should the student expect the event to occur in 60 trials? Would the student prefer a $1/15$ chance of winning $100, or a $3/10$ chance of winning $20? Ask the student to explain his or choice. Encourage accurate, meaningful use of mathematical terms.

Making Predictions and Interpreting Data

One way to make predictions is to treat a set of data as a sample and make a projection based upon those results. If 87 out of the first 145 students voted for Dina Jackson for class president, is she likely to win after all 350 students have voted? There are several ways to calculate this. If the student is not sure how to proceed, encourage exploration and efforts to organize his or her guesses. A more advanced student might be expected to directly solve this question with a proportion or unit equation. A better approach for your student would be to make a table of successive estimates.

Another way to make a prediction is to identify a trendline. Even graphs without a straight line might show a trend that is generally upward or downward. By visually finding the average of high and low points on a graph, a trendline can be drawn to show the general direction of the data. By extending this line, predictions can be made beyond the available data.

Interpreting data requires good number sense and knowledge of mathematical terms. Beyond the accuracy of the math, the interpretation of data requires an evaluation of the reasonableness or appropriateness of the conclusions. Teens grow quickly, so a mathematical projection of growth during the adult years based only on that fast-growth period would not be accurate. If one company makes profits at a greater rate than another company, it isn't necessarily making more money.

> **Helpful Hint:**
> When presenting a new concept let the student look over and think about the material. Be patient while he or she asks questions.

DATA ANALYSIS, STATISTICS, AND PROBABILITY

Activities

1. Help the student practice probability. Put some colored markers or marbles on the table. Count the number of marbles of each color (two or three of each is good). Put all the marbles into a bag and mix them up. Ask the student what would be the probability of drawing a red marble (or blue or other color). The correct answer will be the number of red marbles compared to the total number of marbles. For example, if there are three reds and a total of 12 marbles (including the reds), then the probability of drawing a red marble is ³⁄₁₂, or ¼.

   Have the student draw a marble from the bag 24 times and record the outcomes. Replace the marble after each draw. How many times was a red marble drawn? How many did the student expect to be red?

2. Give your student the following trendline exercise. During a school election, the voting data by class was 13 for Dina out of 22 students in the first class, 14 out of 23 in the next, 13 out of 23 in the next, 15 out of 25 in the next, 15 out of 24 in the next, and 17 out of 28 in the last. The votes for Dina totaled 87 out of 145. Have the student place the total votes on the vertical axis and the number of classes voting on the horizontal axis. The vertical axis should be labeled with numbers 0 to 145. Help the student decide which increment to use (an increment of 5 would require 29 lines on the graph paper.) The horizontal axis should number from 1 to 6. For each class on the horizontal axis, record the corresponding total of votes for Dina. After the first class, she had 13 votes. After the second class, she had a total of 27 votes. After the third class, she had a total of 40 votes. Have the student continue marking the total known votes for Dina. Have the student connect the points with a solid line. Ask the student to look at the first mark and the last mark. Have the student draw a straight, dotted line between the first point and the last point so that half of the solid line is above the dotted line and half is below.

3. Charting the sunrise is another activity that will reinforce the idea that a line graph shows change over time. First, make a table for the student that is appropriate for charting the time of sunrise in your area for a given period of time (start with three weeks). The table should include a column for the date as well as the time for each sunrise. Show the student how to find the time of each sunrise in an almanac. (Try www.almanac.com for a great version of *The Old Farmer's Almanac*.) Have the student complete the table. When it is complete, ask the student to create a line graph using the information. The line graph must have a title and the appropriate labels. Repeat the same process with the sunrise times for another season. Have the student compare the two graphs. Are the days getting longer or shorter? Does the sun rise earlier or later in the winter? Make sure the child supports his or her answers with evidence from the graphs.

Date	Time of Sunrise
August 4, 2000	6:06 am
August 5, 2000	6:07 am
August 6, 2000	6:08 am

Time of Sunrise in Summer

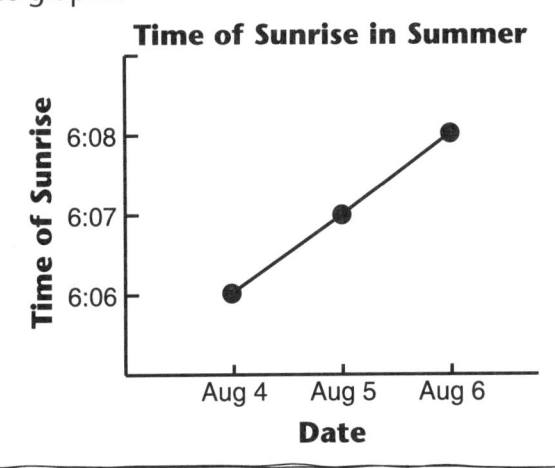

Name _____   Pretest

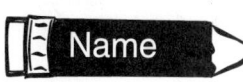

Data Analysis, Statistics, and Probability

1 Find the average. _____

55, 24, 68, 77, 66, 46

2 John wanted to keep a record of his math test scores on a graph. He wanted to allow for a range of scores from 60 to 100. If his graph has 9 lines, how many points should each line represent?

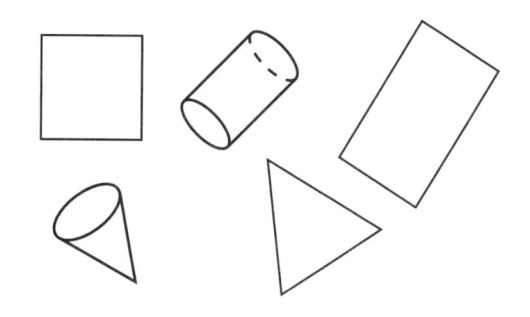

_____

3 If one of the shapes to the left is chosen randomly, what is the probability that it will have four corners?

_____

4 If the shape selected in Question 3 is replaced each time, how many shapes with four corners would you expect to choose after 40 choices? _____

5 Draw a bar graph showing the following information about favorite foods in Mrs. Peterson's class. Use the back of this paper.

Favorite Foods		
pizza	|||| |||| ||||	14
hamburgers	|||| |||	8
steak			1
pasta	||	2

© 2001 Frank Schaffer Publications, Inc.   FS122133 The Tutor's Handbook: Math Grade 5

Pizza Palace

One week, Big Mike's Pizza Palace sold 18 pepperoni, 2 anchovy, 22 combination, 12 sausage, and 6 garlic chicken pizzas. Make a pictograph to show this information; then answer the questions below.

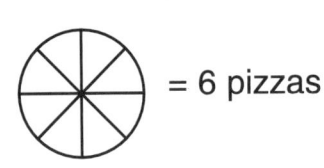

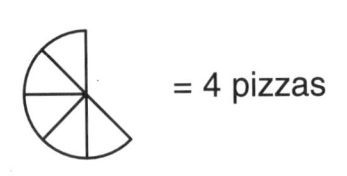

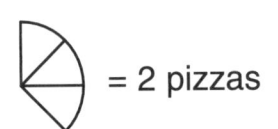

Pizza Sales

= 6 pizzas

= 4 pizzas

= 2 pizzas

Pepperoni   Anchovy   Combination   Sausage   Garlic Chicken

Types of Pizza

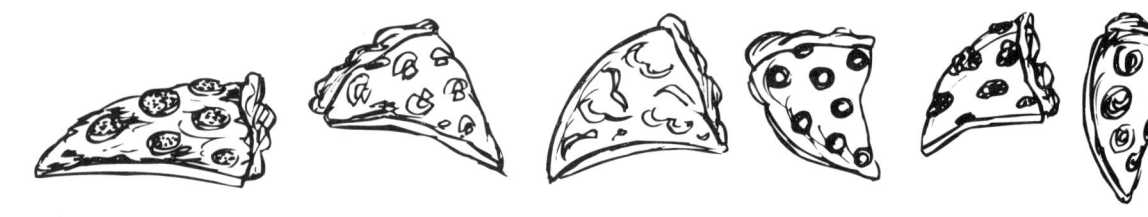

1 Find the average number of pizzas sold. Draw a horizontal line on your graph to show the average. Which types of pizza sold more than the average?

2 If a new customer came in to order a pizza and you had no way of knowing what type he liked, what would be the likelihood (probability) of his ordering garlic chicken?

3 Would you say that a customer who orders garlic chicken pizza is an average customer? Why or why not?

Number Roll

For the following experiment, you will need a pair of dice. Roll both dice 30 times and keep a tally of the sum of the numbers you roll.

Sum of Numbers rolled	Tallies
2	
3	
4	
5	
6	
7	
8	
9	
10	
11	
12	

1 How many 7s did you roll? _____

2 How many 7s would you expect to roll if you rolled the dice 60 times? _____

3 When rolling a pair of dice, the smallest number you can roll is 2, and there is only one way to get 2. A total of 3 can be made in two ways: a 1 on the first die and a 2 on the second, or a 2 on the first and a 1 on the second. A total of 4 can be made three ways. When rolling a pair of dice, how many ways are there to make all of the totals 2–12? _____

4 On your chart, how many ways are there to make a sum of 7? _____

Data Analysis, Statistics, and Probability

Graphs and Averages

Leonard takes a multiplication test each day in his math class. He has earned the following scores: 74, 71, 75, 77, 76, 80, 79, 82, 84, 82, 85, 87, 88, 87, 90, 91, 93, 90, 95, and 96.

1 Make a line graph to show Leonard's progress.

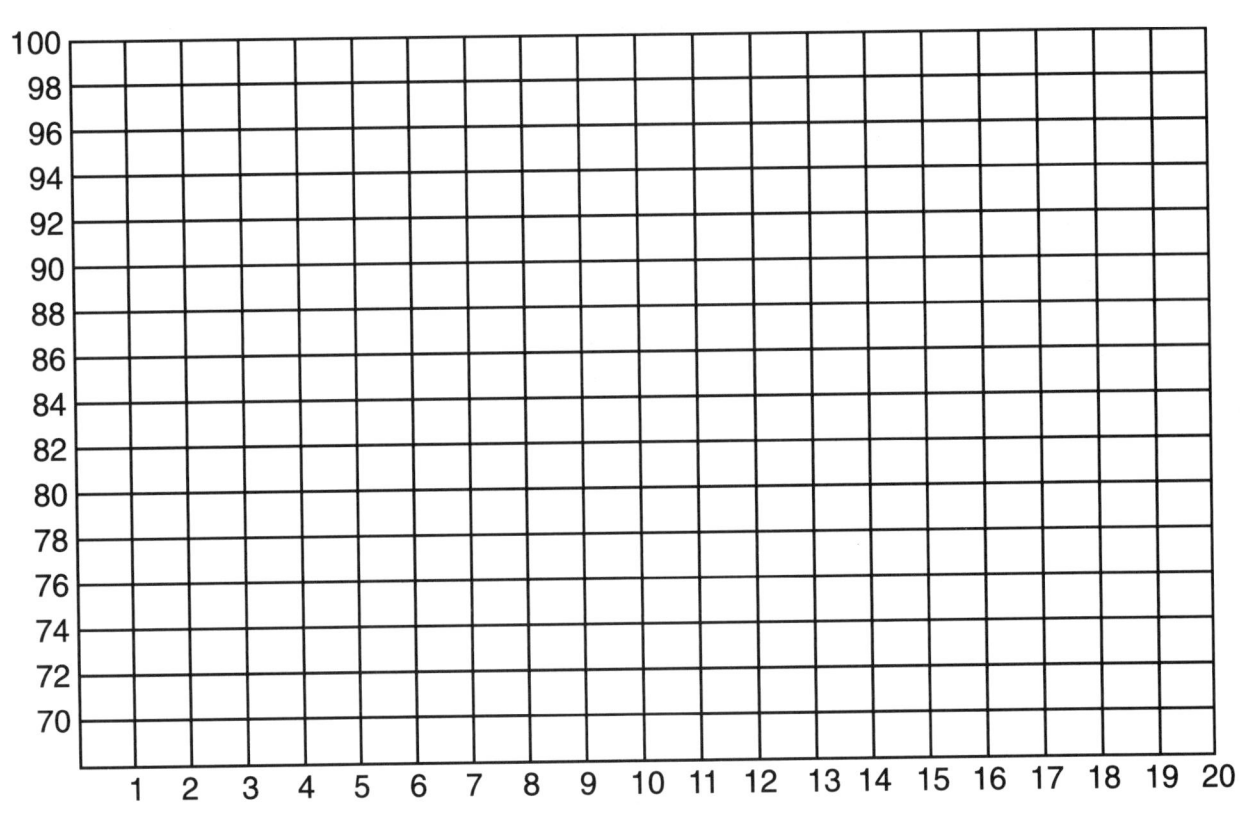

[Grid with y-axis from 70 to 100 in increments of 2, and x-axis from 1 to 20]

2 About how much is Leonard improving each day? _____

3 Will Leonard continue to improve at this rate over the next 10 tests? Why or why not?

_____
_____
_____

4 Determine Leonard's average test score. _____

© 2001 Frank Schaffer Publications, Inc.

48 reproducible

FS122133 The Tutor's Handbook: Math Grade 5

Data Analysis, Statistics, and Probability

1 Find the average number of days per month in a leap year.

_____ days per month

2 Tamara wants to try out for the basketball team. Each day she practices for 30 minutes. The following table shows the number of jump shots Tamara made during one week of practice. Make a line graph showing Tamara's progress.

Practice Day	Shots Made
1	5
2	7
3	10
4	13
5	14
6	16
7	17

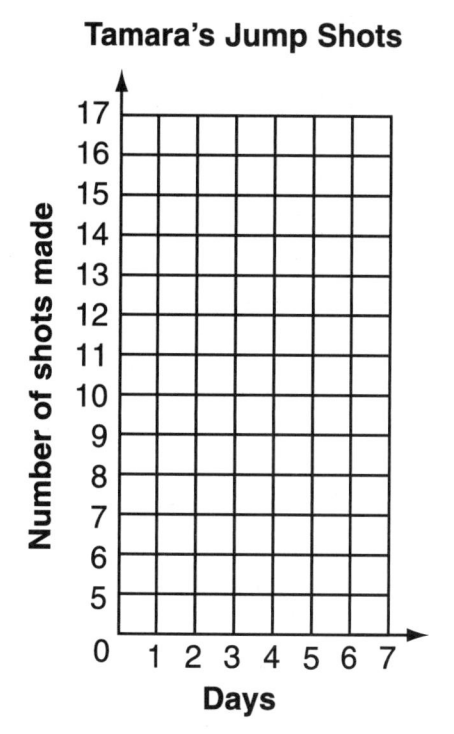

Tamara's Jump Shots

(graph with y-axis: Number of shots made, 0-17; x-axis: Days, 0-7)

3 If you stopped in front of one of the houses to the right at random, what is the probability that it would be a two-story house with three windows?

_____

4 If this pattern of houses were repeated 35 times, how many two-story houses would there be altogether? _____

5 Cindy has scored a total of 415 points on her last 5 tests. What score would you expect her to get on her next test? _____

PROBLEM SOLVING

Unlike arithmetic problems, such as 5 + 4 = ___, in which there are obvious computations to perform, word problems suggest no immediately obvious methods to solve them. Developing proficiency in basic computation is a warmup for the actual application of math to practical problems. Problem solving requires proficient understanding and use of the language of mathematics and the ability to organize information.

The problems on the following pages do not always provide clues as to which operations to perform. While word problems in previous sections of this book were related to the skill presented in each section, the problems here are mixed and may require any of the skills studied so far.

Problem-Solving Strategies

To solve word problems, the student will need to know how to restate them in his or her own words. Listen to the student carefully to determine whether his or her description shows an understanding of what is being asked. If the student doesn't know where to begin, ask him or her to restate the problem again.

The student needs to know the vocabulary of math—for example, the difference between *numeral* and *digit* and the difference between phrases like *twice more than* and *twice as many*.

Helpful Hint: In math class, the student may have learned a problem-solving method that differs from yours. Let him or her master that way first and then use the different approach to build understanding.

Knowing how to create tables, charts, and pictures to organize and make sense of the provided information will also help the student solve word problems.

Use a highlighter to mark the important information in a problem. This way the student can focus on the relevant data. Teach the child about key words that can give clues to what needs to be done to solve the problem.

Confidence

It is important to help the student build confidence in problem solving. A student who is new to the task of problem solving may at first toss up his or her hands and declare that it is impossible. Let the student know that this is an experience we have all had and that the first skill to master is patience. One way to get "unstuck" is to back up and look at the problem from another angle. Often, it is helpful to begin by having the student state anything that is known, even if it is obvious.

Beware of helping the student too much at this stage. Problem solving takes time, and it is easy for the time-conscious adult to want to move things along by helping out. If the student seems to ask questions in order to avoid figuring a problem out, ask him or her why that is the appropriate operation.

Reading Word Problems

Word problems are more difficult to read than other types of reading. If the student is not a strong reader, you may wish to help by first reading the problem to him or her, then reading it together, then having the student read it alone. Afterward, question the student on what was read. Be sure that the student understands the meaning of the words.

Process

Discuss with the student the importance of the process of problem solving. Problem solving is quite different from basic operations, measurement, and geometry. The student will be eager to get to the answer and may at first become frustrated by the ambiguity of how to proceed.

Problem Solving

Solve each problem.

1. To encourage him to save, Terrel's father added $0.75 to Terrel's savings account for each dollar that Terrel put in. Terrel's savings account has grown to $26.25. How much money has Terrel's father added?

   answer: _____

2. The perimeter of the rectangle to the right is 48 inches. The area is 143 square inches. What are the dimensions?

   answer: _____

3. George saves $10.00 every three days. At this rate, how much will he save in ten days?

   answer: _____

4. $\frac{3}{8}$ of what number is 9?

   answer: _____

5. If you multiply Paula's age by 3 and subtract 3, you get 33. How old is Paula?

   answer: _____

6. Mr. Turtle walks at 1 m.p.h. His friend, Mr. Hare, can run at 30 m.p.h. They are going to race a distance of one mile. Mr. Turtle gets a half hour head start. If the hare runs continuously, who will win the race?

   answer: _____

Name _____

Problem Solving

School Days

Solve each problem.

1. Joe and Pedro walk to school together every morning. Joe's age last year was twice Pedro's age now. The sum of their ages is 19. What are their ages now?

answer: _____

2. The school store sold 39 pencils this week. Two-thirds of those pencils were sold on Monday. One-tenth of the pencils sold were yellow. How many pencils were sold on Monday?

answer: _____

3. Penelope needs to buy a notebook. The school store is open before school and after school. The hours are 7:30 a.m. to 8:15 a.m. and 3:00 p.m. to 4:00 p.m. How much longer is the school store open after school than before school?

answer: _____

4. Marco has run out of notebook paper. He can buy a package of 100 sheets for $2.50 at the school store. He can buy a package of 1000 sheets for $10.00 at the office supply store. Which store has the better price per sheet?

answer: _____

5. Jeff is the towel monitor in the school gym. When a towel is wet, it weighs about 18 ounces. When dry, the towel weighs about 12 ounces. How much more does the towel weigh when wet?

answer: _____

Note to tutor: For additional practice have the student highlight the necessary information and draw a line through the unnecessary information.

© 2001 Frank Schaffer Publications, Inc.   FS122133 The Tutor's Handbook: Math Grade 5

Word Problems

1 A calorie is the amount of energy needed to raise the temperature of 1 liter of water by 1 degree centigrade. How many calories would it take to raise the temperature of 75 centiliters of water by 3 degrees?

answer: _____

2 A piece of paper measures 8½" x 11". If a one-inch margin is left blank around all edges of the paper, what is the area of the paper that will be written on?

answer: _____

3 If four quarters weigh one ounce, what would be the monetary value of 6 lb, 11 oz of quarters?

answer: _____

Problem Solving

Missing Information

Write the missing information.

1 Juanita needs to mail a package. The package weighs 6 pounds and 3 ounces. How much will it cost to mail the package?

_____

_____

2 Carlotta, Jason, and Tran will put their savings together to buy a scooter. Carlotta has saved $\frac{1}{3}$ more than Jason and Tran. How much have they saved altogether?

_____

_____

3 Victoria is planting a garden. She can plant 5 seeds in each row of her garden. She has already seeded $\frac{2}{5}$ of the rows in the garden. How many rows does she have left to seed?

_____

_____

4 George and Devon have brought their dogs to the park. Devon's dog can catch a stick by jumping 6 feet in the air. How much higher can Devon's dog jump than George's dog?

_____

_____

5 Sheila is having a birthday party. Her mother has allowed her to invite $\frac{3}{5}$ of all her friends to the party. How many friends is Sheila inviting to her party?

_____

_____

Name _____   Posttest

Problem Solving

1) Ana and Carlos opened a lemonade stand. They decided that Ana would get $\frac{5}{6}$ of the profit and Carlos would get $\frac{3}{8}$. What is wrong with this arrangement?

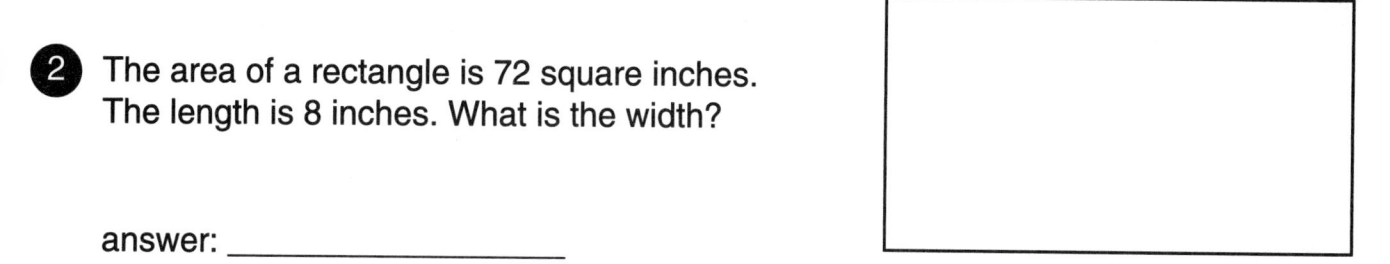

_____

_____

2) The area of a rectangle is 72 square inches. The length is 8 inches. What is the width?

answer: _____

3) In how many ways can 3 books and 2 interchangeable bookends be arranged?

answer: _____

4) Cal noticed that the largest sum he could make by adding any 3 numbers on the current calendar month was 84. What month was it?

answer: _____

5) Put the numerals 1, 2, 4, and 8 in the blanks below so that the value of each digit will be $\frac{1}{20}$ of the value of the digit to the left.

____ . ____ ____ ____

© 2001 Frank Schaffer Publications, Inc.   FS122133 The Tutor's Handbook: Math Grade 5

Let's Review

Solve.

1) 638
   × 53

2) 7,481,271
   +2,134,579

3) 230,005,200
   −   4,503,650

4) $7 \frac{16}{25}$
   $- 3 \frac{6}{25}$

5) 638.6 ÷ 31 = _____

6) 1 − (5 × 0.065) = _____

7) $\frac{7}{10} + \frac{4}{5} =$

8) $17 \frac{3}{4}$
   $+ 5 \frac{1}{2}$

9) Write this number: four hundred thousandths. _____

10) Which fraction is not an equivalent of $\frac{7}{8}$? $\frac{56}{64}$ $\frac{21}{32}$ $\frac{63}{72}$ $\frac{28}{32}$

11) What part of the rectangle is shaded?

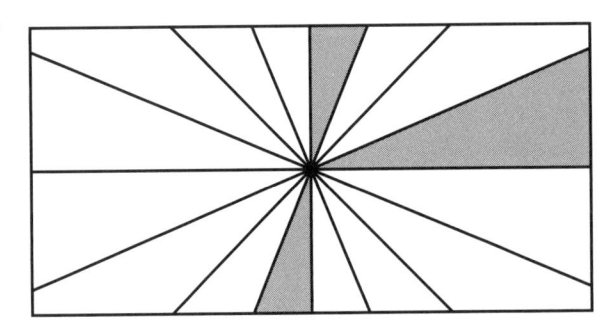

_____

Name _____ Patterns

Let's Review

1 What are the next two numbers in this sequence?

17, 38, 59, _____, _____

2 What number, when subtracted from three times the number, equals 3? _____

3 How many lines will it take to make the next figure in this series? _____

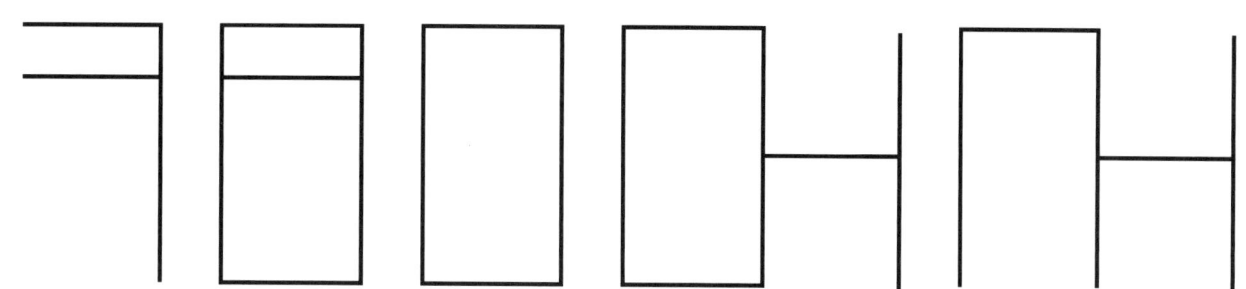

4 What number times itself equals 2,025?

_____

5 How many two-digit numbers have both 3 and 7 as factors?

_____

Name _____ Geometry

Let's Review

Write the name of each shape.

1. _____

2. _____

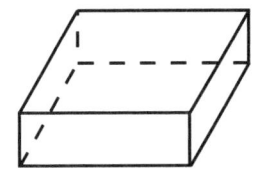

3. _____

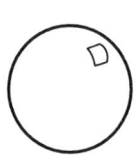

4. _____

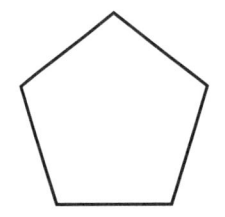

5. _____

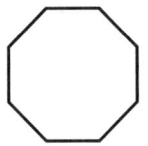

6. _____

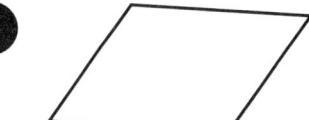

Plot each point on the grid. Mark each point with the letter.

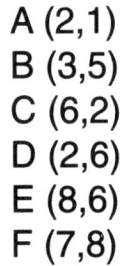

7.
A (2,1)
B (3,5)
C (6,2)
D (2,6)
E (8,6)
F (7,8)

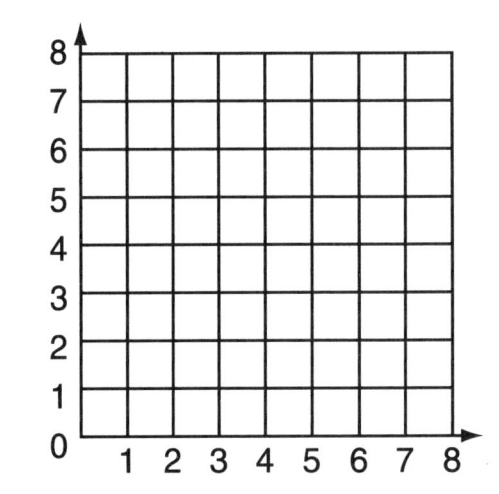

Name _____ Measurement

Let's Review

Solve.

1) 8 yards 1 foot 6 inches
    − 5 yards 1 foot 8 inches
    _____

Find the area and perimeter of this figure.

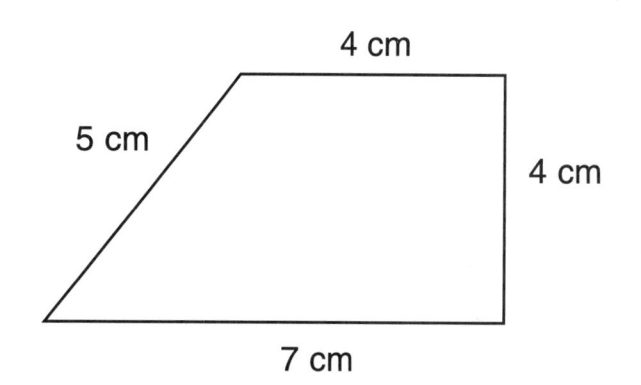

2) Area = _____

3) Perimeter = _____

(figure: trapezoid with top 4 cm, left slant 5 cm, right side 4 cm, bottom 7 cm)

Find each answer.

4) 650 cm = _____ m

5) 3 gallons, 1 quart, 1 pint = _____ cups

6) Who do you know who might be .0185 hm tall? _____

7) 75 inches = _____ yards

8) Which of these figures has an area that is 2/3 of the area of another one of the figures?

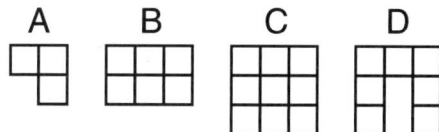

    A   B   C   D

9) Make a rectangle that has a perimeter equal to the length of this line. Use the back of this paper.

Let's Review

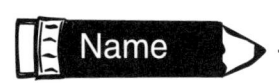

1 Find the average of 16, 28, 40, and 27. _____

2 Find the average of the first four multiples of 28. _____

3 If a month of the year is chosen at random, what is the probability that the name of the month will have an r in it? _____

4 Complete the bar graph using the information provided in the tally chart.

Favorite Subject in School		
Math	ⵜⵜ ⵜⵜ |||	13
Language Arts	ⵜⵜ |||	8
Science	ⵜⵜ |||	8
Physical Education	ⵜⵜ ||	7

Favorite Subject in School

Number of Students (0–14)

Math | Language Arts | Science | Physical Education

Favorite Subject

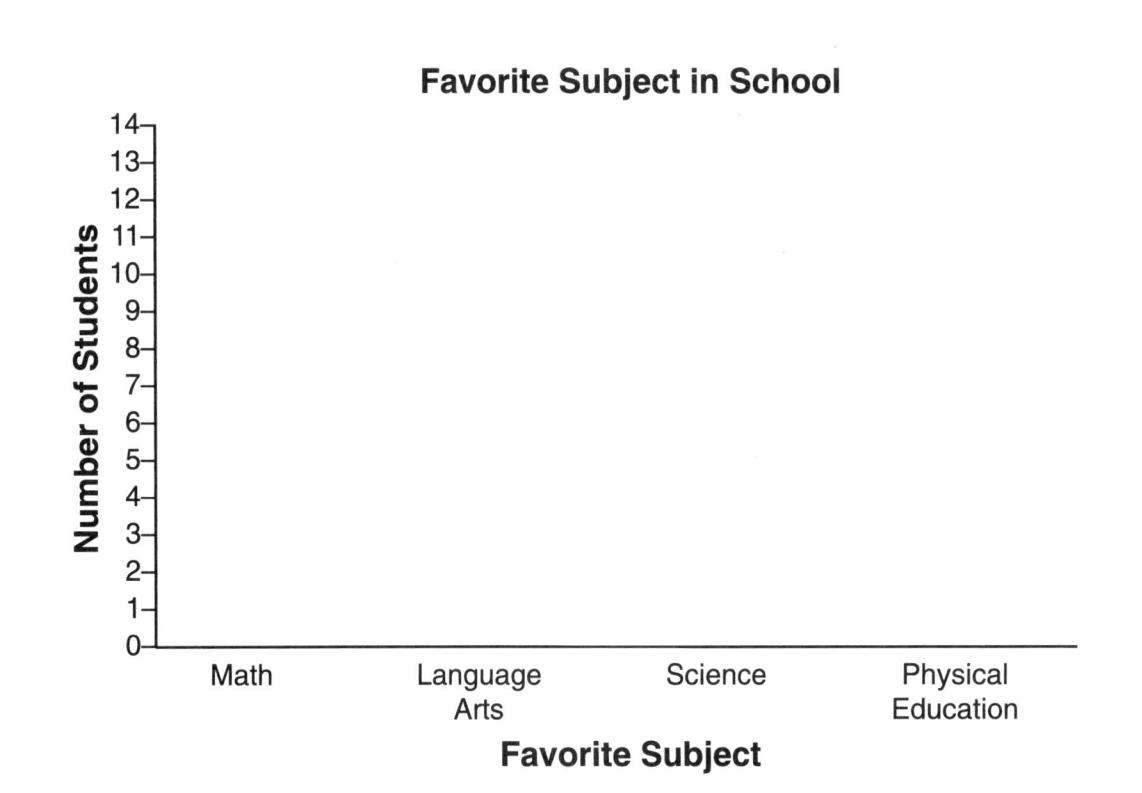

Let's Review

Solve each problem.

1) The area of the rectangle is 120 cm². What is the perimeter?

12 cm

_____

2) An astronaut will travel 327,912 miles on an experimental rocket. If she had to make the trip 16 times, how many miles will she have traveled? _____

3) In the first inning of a baseball game, 6 batters stepped up to bat. The pitcher struck out 2 batters. Three batters got hits. One batter grounded out. What fraction of the batters got hits? What percentage is that? _____

4) Jerry has 16 ounces of grape juice in his lunch. Teresa has 1 cup of orange juice in her lunch.

Who has more juice? _____

5) A bird flew 10 miles on the first day of its migration to the south. It flew 2 more miles the second day than on the first day. Each day the bird flew 2 more miles than the previous day. How many total miles had the bird flown by the fourth day?

_____

Student _____ Final

Student Survey

Use this survey at the end of each semester or when the tutoring is complete. Compare the student's responses on this survey with his or her responses on the beginning survey.

1 How have your skills in math changed since we began this program?

2 How would you compare your math skills with those of other students your age?

3 When we started this program, you said that math (was, was not) one of your favorite classes. Has that changed any? Why?

4 What is the best part and what is the worst part about math?

5 When we started this tutoring, you said that you thought the tutoring would be. . . . What do you think about the tutoring now?

6 Tutor's observations:

Answers

Page 15
1. 6,490,985
2. 503
3. 6¼
4. 24,336
5. ⁹⁄₁₆
6. ⅓, ⅜, ⁵⁄₁₂
7. 3½
8. Answers will vary but may include two of the following: ⅝, ⁹⁄₁₂, ¹²⁄₁₆, ¹⁵⁄₂₀

Page 16
1. 4.495
2. 2.7
3. 6.861
4. 30.80
5. 200.020
6. 0.18
7. ⁴⁵⁄₁₀₀
8. 3,146

Page 17
1. ⁶⁄₇
2. 1¹³⁄₁₄
3. ⅔
4. ⅓ ⅜ ¾
5. ⁹⁄₁₀
6. 1¹⁄₁₂
7. 2⅖
8. ¼
9. 0.25

Page 18
1. 37.385
2. 7.5
3. 34,713
4. 604
5. 1⅚
6. 4,999,976
7. 1⁷⁄₂₄
8. 936,482
9. 4⁵⁄₁₀
10. ⁵⁄₁₂
11. 4,307.81

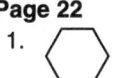

Page 22
1. (hexagon)
2. 64
3. 31.250
4. 5
5. The letter L

Page 23
1. CF, DE
2. 436
3. The fifth term
4. Answers will vary
5. Answers will vary

Page 24
1. 12 possible arrangements
2. 16
3. 2 (ace, beg)
4. 202

Page 25
1. 64
2. The starting number is being multiplied by 2.5.; 50, 80
3. 171, 323, 494, 646, 969

Page 26
1. ¾
2. 82, 99
3. 16
4. 1
5. 49

Page 29
1. pentagon
2. cylinder
3. octagon
4. Answers will vary
5. C
6. (4,5)
7. A

Page 30
1. d
2. a
3. b
4. c
5. rectangular prism
6. cube
7. 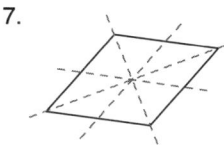 (figure)
8. 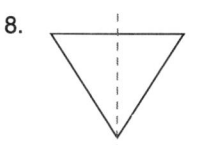 (figure)

Page 31
1. (8,6)
2. C, F
3. (0,7)
4. 12
5. 34
6. 39

Page 32
1. b
2. a
3. c
4. flip
5. turn
6. slide
7. turn

Page 33
1. pentagon
2. quadrilateral
3. hexagon
4. sphere
5. pyramid
6. rectangular prism
7. 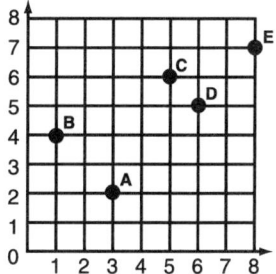 (coordinate grid with points A–E)

Page 37
1. .45
2. 1⅔
3. 5 inches
4. b
5. 39 sq. cm
6. 336 cm cubed
7. 12:35 p.m.
8. 18 in.
9. 51.75 sq. cm

Page 38
1. 5,000
2. 1
3. 20
4. 3
5. 80
6. 2.5
7. 8,000
8. 100
9. 30.7
10. 5.275
11. 75
12. 30 cm
13. 150 mm, 15 cm, 1.5 dm, .15 m

Page 39
1. 8 feet 5 inches
2. ¾ foot
3. 78 sq. in.
4. 2 yards 10 inches
5. 1 hr 36 minutes
6. 2 p.m.

Page 40
1. 33⅓
2. 1,000 days
3. 100,000
4. 250 gallons
5. 1 hour 30 minutes
6. 1¼
7. 96 cubes

Page 41
1. d
2. 680
3. 5
4. 38 sq. in.
5. 34 in.
6. 60 cubic cm
7. 6:15 p.m.

Page 45
1. 56
2. 5
3. ⅖
4. 16
5. Answers will vary

Page 46
1. 12, pepperoni and combination
2. ¹⁄₁₀
3. No, because sales of the garlic chicken pizza are below average.

Page 47
1. Answers will vary.
2. Answers will vary but should be twice the answer to the question above.
3. 36

© 2001 Frank Schaffer Publications, Inc.   FS122133 The Tutor's Handbook: Math Grade 5

Answers

Page 48
1. 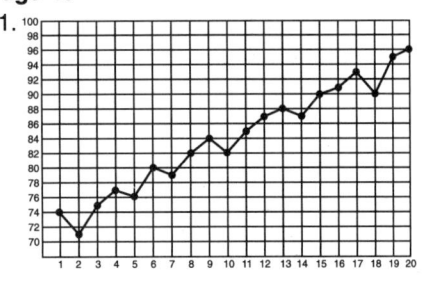 [line graph showing values from about 70 to 96 over points 1–20]
2. Answers will vary (about 1¼ point per day).
3. No, because he will soon have a perfect score.
4. 84.1

Page 49
1. 30.5
2. 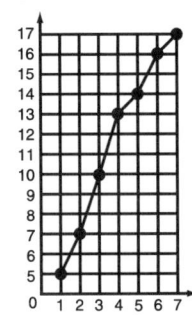 [line graph plotting points from (1,5) up to (7,17)]
3. ⅗
4. 105
5. 83

Page 51
1. $11.25
2. 11 in. x 13 in.
3. $33.33
4. 24
5. 12
6. Mr. Hare

Page 52
1. Joe is 13, Phil is 6.
2. 26
3. 15 minutes
4. office store
5. 6 ounces more

Page 53
1. 2.25 calories
2. 58.5 sq in
3. $107

Page 54
1. the cost of postage
2. how much Jason and Tran saved or how much Carlotta saved
3. how many rows total
4. how high George's dog can jump
5. how many friends Sheila has total

Page 55
1. The fractions add up to more than one whole.
2. 9 inches
3. 12
4. February
5. 8.421

Page 56
1. 33,814
2. 9,615,850
3. 225,501,550
4. 4⅖
5. 20.6
6. 0.675
7. 1½
8. 23¼
9. .00004
10. ²¹⁄₃₂
11. ³⁄₁₆

Page 57
1. 80,101
2. 1.5 or 1½
3. 7
4. 45
5. 4

Page 58
1. cylinder
2. rectangular prism
3. sphere
4. pentagon
5. octagon
6. parallelogram
7. 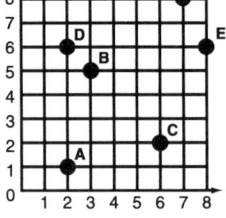 [coordinate grid showing points A(2,1), B(3,5), C(6,2), D(2,6), E(7,6), F(6,8)]

Page 59
1. 2 yards 2 feet 10 inches
2. 22 sq. cm
3. 20 cm
4. 6.5 m
5. 54 cups
6. answers may vary (should be an adult)
7. 2¹⁄₁₂
8. b
9. Answers will vary

Page 60
1. 27.75
2. 70
3. ⅔ or ⁸⁄₁₂
4. 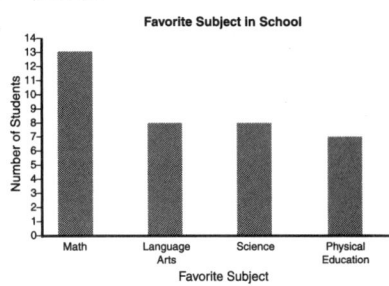 [bar graph "Favorite Subject in School" — Math 13, Language Arts 8, Science 8, Physical Education 7]

Page 61
1. 44 cm
2. 5,246,592 miles
3. ⅗, 50%
4. Jerry
5. 52 miles